DEMOCRACY IN CALIFORNIA

DEMOCRACY IN CALIFORNIA
Politics and Government in the Golden State

Fourth Edition

Brian P. Janiskee and Ken Masugi

ROWMAN & LITTLEFIELD
Lanham • Boulder • New York • London

Executive Editor: Jon Sisk
Associate Editor: Natalie Mandziuk
Senior Marketing Manager: Karin Cholek
Marketing Manager: Deborah Hudson
Production Editor: Elaine McGarraugh
Interior Designer: Rhonda Baker
Cover Designer: Meredith Nelson

Credits and acknowledgments of sources for material or information used with permission appear on the appropriate page within the text.

Published by Rowman & Littlefield
A wholly owned subsidiary of The Rowman & Littlefield Publishing Group, Inc.
4501 Forbes Boulevard, Suite 200, Lanham, Maryland 20706
www.rowman.com

Unit A, Whitacre Mews, 26-34 Stannary Street, London SE11 4AB

British Library Cataloguing in Publication Information Available

Library of Congress Cataloging-in-Publication Data

Janiskee, Brian P., 1967-
  Democracy in California : politics and government in the Golden State / Brian P. Janiskee and Ken Masugi. — Fourth edition.
    pages cm
  Includes bibliographical references and index.
  ISBN 978-1-4422-4751-2 (cloth : alk. paper) — ISBN 978-1-4422-4753-6 (pbk. : alk. paper) — ISBN 978-1-4422-4752-9 (electronic) 1. California—Politics and government—Textbooks. I. Masugi, Ken. II. Title.
  JK8716.J36 2015
  320.4974—dc23

                                                              2015010097

Printed in the United States of America

Contents

Preface to the Fourth Edition

> To instruct democracy, if possible to reanimate its beliefs, to purify its mores, to regulate its movements, to substitute little by little the science of affairs for its inexperience, and knowledge of its true interests for its blind instincts; to adapt its government to time and place; to modify it according to circumstances and men: such is the first duty imposed on those who direct society in our day.[1]

WERE IT AN INDEPENDENT NATION, California would be the eighth-largest economy in the world, just below Brazil and slightly above Russia.[2] It would also be the world's strangest democracy. The institutions of federalism and the separation of powers, developed by the U.S. Constitution to enable a large representative democracy to exist, do not characterize California democracy. By contrast, California has a weak, fragmented executive, and local governments depend on the state government in Sacramento for major portions of their budgets. There is no "federal analogy" by which California counties can be compared with American states under federalism.

Often noted as well is the ethnic composition of California, which would make it a major Latino nation. (It also has the largest percentage of Asians and Asian Americans of any continental state.) But diversity and prosperity do not alone explain California's government and why Californians govern the way they do. Such an understanding requires an examination of California history, political traditions, and political character. It is the third-largest state, 770 miles long and 250 miles wide at its most distant points. Mountains, deserts, forests, beaches, farmland, and federally owned land (almost half of the total) bound the habitable areas that contain nearly forty million people, about 12 percent of the U.S. population. California remains an attraction for settlers—as it was during the Gold Rush and is for those from abroad today. Do its Pacific and Mexican borders mean an opening to exotic cultures, or are they an invitation to disturbing alien ways? Do they signal opportunity or the need for self-defense?[3]

California's geographic separation from the United States, and the unique circumstances of its entry into the Union via the Compromise of 1850, has enabled an independent political character to develop. A major example of this independence is the power, by majority popular vote, to amend the state constitution. These initiative, referendum, and recall powers reflect that defining, still-evolving movement within American politics known as Progressivism, which sought to rid politics of corruption by subjecting it to a new, professionalized, and scientific political process. In many regards, from its professional legislature to its centralization of power in Sacramento, from its mood swings on dealing with race and ethnicity to the initiative and referendum, the Golden State has embodied the spirit and reality of Progressivism. Throughout *Democracy in California* we will note the Progressivist character of California political life, but our primary purpose is to explain California's governmental institutions and how their dynamics affect our lives, for better and for worse. How do we make sense of California politics? How does it reflect democracy's blind instincts, its true interests, or its seemingly boundless opportunities?

In this ambitious effort, as our title reflects, we are guided by Alexis de Tocqueville's classic, *Democracy in America*. What might a student of Tocqueville or, more important, of American government say on examining California today? We emphasize that our text presupposes no familiarity whatsoever with the classic text by this nineteenth-century French political theorist and statesman (1805–1859); our text stands by itself as a succinct guide to California politics and is intended for the reader who has some basic familiarity with American government and politics.

We begin with elements of Tocqueville's teaching that seem to characterize many Californians (and other Americans): their indifference to politics, their love of novelty, their desire for wealth and status, and their love of freedom balanced with resentment of those they perceive as privileged. From our first chapter on the diversity of California, as Tocqueville might have perceived it, we develop other Tocquevillean themes in subsequent chapters. The two tasks reinforce each other, making possible a more compelling and, frankly, more interesting understanding of California's political life than hitherto available. At the end of each chapter, we highlight "real-world" issues taken from the headlines. While it is necessary for the properly educated citizen to understand the mechanics of government, it is not sufficient. Citizens must see the vital connection between the *form* of government and the *substance* of everyday political life. It is our hope that the reader will understand and assess the workings of California politics and government and, with encouragement, become one of Tocqueville's engaged citizens.

While the final manuscript is a mutual product, the general division of labor in the manuscript's development was as follows: Brian Janiskee wrote chapters 3–7, 9, and 10; and Ken Masugi wrote the introduction and chapters 1, 2, and 8.

We thank the University of Chicago Press for permission to quote extensively from its edition of *Democracy in America*, which was edited and translated by Harvey C. Mansfield and Delba Winthrop. We are grateful to the University of California Press for permission to reprint material from Mark Baldassare, *California at the Millennium: The Changing Social and Political Landscape*. We also wish to thank Viking-Penguin for its kind permission to quote from Richard Rodriguez, *Days of Obligation: Arguments with My Mexican Father*, and Simon and Schuster for its kind permission to quote from Victor Davis Hanson, *The Land Was Everything*.

We are grateful for the support we received in the preparation of this book. Daniel C. Palm of Azusa Pacific University, Richard Reeb of Barstow College, Althea Nagai of NagaiLerner Associates, and John J. Pitney Jr., of Claremont McKenna College read the entire manuscript and offered several helpful suggestions. Ralph Rossum of Claremont McKenna College gave help and encouragement.

We thank our colleagues and friends at California State University, San Bernardino, for their support and encouragement: Mark Clark, Meredith Conroy, Edward Erler, Antony Field, Alemayehu Mariam, and Scot Zentner. I offer special thanks to our department secretary, Marilyn Gareis, who provided crucial support throughout the course of this project. We also thank our graduate assistant, Aaron Holmes, who worked tirelessly to update vital facts and sources for this new edition. We thank Jon Sisk, Natalie Mandziuk, Elaine McGarraugh, and all those at Rowman & Littlefield who made this project possible. We thank the Claremont Institute for their professional support of previous editions of this text. Without the support of the Claremont Institute, this project would not have been possible. Howard Ahmanson, senior counselor of the institute's Center for Local Government, inspired us to write this book. Claremont Institute President Brian Kennedy encouraged each step of the process. We hope our book reflects the rigor and vigor Harry V. Jaffa displayed in his investigation of equality in the American political tradition. Professor Jaffa passed away at ninety-six on January 10, 2015, as this new edition was being prepared. We are among the many that have been inspired, challenged, and awakened by his teachings.

Brian Janiskee wishes to thank his wife, Jennifer, and daughters, Alexandra, Katherine, and Mary. In addition, he wishes to thank Professor Carol Weissert of Florida State University for encouraging his interest in state politics. Ken Masugi wishes to thank his wife, Althea, his daughter, Vera, and her late grandmother Mary. The support and understanding of our families during the completion of this manuscript was more than we could have reasonably expected.

We remain indebted to the late Thomas B. Silver, former president of the Claremont Institute, to whom this book is dedicated. His assistance was not merely self-interest properly understood, to use a Tocquevillean concept. Tom passed away suddenly on December 26, 2001. He will be remembered as a friend, colleague, and ardent champion of the principles of the American Founding.

Introduction

I confess that in America I saw more than America. I sought there an image of democracy itself, of its penchants, its character, its prejudices, its passions; I wanted to become acquainted with it if only to know at least what we ought to hope or fear from it.[1]

A LEXIS DE TOCQUEVILLE (1805–1859) wrote one of the most intriguing books ever published about America and our politics. Even after over 170 years, his two-volume *Democracy in America* remains, in the view of generations of readers and leading scholars, "the best book ever written on democracy and the best book written on America."[2]

Tocqueville was a French aristocrat who toured America for a little more than nine months in 1831–1832. Not merely a scholar learned in philosophy, history, and literature, he was also a patriot devoted to politics who later served briefly as minister of foreign affairs during the Second French Republic (1848). Originally, Tocqueville wrote to educate his fellow Frenchmen to the ways of democracy, but his book would make its greatest impression on generations of Americans, beginning with its publication and immediate translation. His seven-hundred-page work met with great praise immediately upon its publication, and it continues to be issued in new translations and scholarly editions. His brilliance casts light on topics ranging from education to the role of women, from the influence of money on our character to race relations.[3]

After a civil war, industrialization, immigration, world wars, and a civil rights revolution, this claim of enduring wisdom may appear to be exaggerated. But Tocqueville would have a penetrating explanation for all of these great events and how they shaped the essential character of America and its people. His famous predictions (e.g., of the Cold War division of the world between Russia and America) may be taken to signify his understanding of America. He seems to have put his finger on the heart of what it means to be an American. Even beyond his astounding predictions, what makes him such a great teacher is his ability to speak frankly and persuasively about both our faults and our virtues. One can ransack his book for striking sayings, but that reduces its depth to its surface.

Moreover, even when Tocqueville's 170-year-old analyses seem outdated— for example, in changes to race relations and the place of religion in civic affairs—we have nonetheless a comparison with other eras in America, which can be instructive concerning what we have gained and what we have lost over the years. Are we a freer people than we were fifty years ago? Is there more equality, more liberty, more patriotism? The greatness of Tocqueville's book and its enduring vitality over time rest squarely on its ability to counter our faults. Tocqueville remains ever our teacher, even when we fail to pay attention.

So what can Tocqueville teach us? Consider some Californian and American traits that at first don't seem related to politics but that we believe go a long way in explaining California. Americans reveal an indifference to politics, a love of wealth, a craving for novelty, an unhealthy individualism, and a jealousy about their equality that can overwhelm even their regard for liberty. Thus, Californians are Americans—Tocqueville's Americans.

Consider the much-bemoaned American indifference to politics. In California less than 31 percent of all eligible voters bothered to vote in the November 2014 elections, and voting is considered a minimal sign of involvement in politics.[4] But, according to Tocqueville, we were always a people too busy for politics. And Tocqueville also noted how Americans are in fact political, in ways more significant than voting—for example, in being an active member of a PTA or aiding a charity.[5] Thus, in being indifferent to politics in the narrow sense of holding office, we are being very American—but being overly American in this sense can undo us as a nation. Tocqueville recognized that the American is a complex being—and the Californian no less so—and extremes in any direction can lead to change for the worse.

> Private life is so active in democratic times, so agitated, so filled with desires and work, that hardly any energy or leisure remains to each man for political life. . . . That such penchants are not invincible I shall not deny, since my principal goal in writing this book has been to combat them.[6]

A "private life . . . filled with desires and work." It becomes too easy for the Californian to confuse work—that is, the money it brings—with the purpose of life.

I do not know a country where the love of money holds a larger place in the heart of man and where they profess a more profound scorn for the theory of the permanent equality of goods.[7]

Our desire for wealth goes hand in hand with our desire for novelty. Americans want the latest clothing styles, cars, fast-food crazes, and smartphones. But how new must the new be? Should our laws change as quickly as the features at the local movie theater?

> The American inhabits a land of prodigies, around him everything is constantly moving, and each movement seems to be progress. The idea of the new is therefore intimately bound in his mind to the idea of the better. Nowhere does he perceive any boundary that nature can have set to the efforts of man; in his eyes, what is not is what has not yet been attempted.
>
> The American taken randomly will therefore be a man ardent in his desires, enterprising, adventurous—above all, an innovator. This spirit is in fact found in all his works; he introduces it into his political laws, his religious doctrines, his theories of social economy, his private industry; he brings it with him everywhere, into the depth of the woods as into the heart of the towns.[8]

But this quest for wealth and for innovation—recall the Gold Rush—has consequences for the way one treats one's family, neighbors, friends, and society in general.

> In the West one can observe democracy reaching its furthest limit. In those states, improvised in a way by fortune, the inhabitants arrived only yesterday on the soil they occupy. They hardly know one another, and each is ignorant of the past of his closest neighbor. . . . The new states of the West already have inhabitants; society does not yet exist there.[9]

Tocqueville would later describe this condition as individualism, an unhealthy condition he linked to democratic times.[10] Isolated from one another, men and women lose their ability to act together for common purposes such as improvement of the local schools. They thus become more dependent on governmental authority. The Americans of Tocqueville's era were guided by a religious faith that gave men and women the moral framework that led to strong families, law-abiding behavior, a consistent work ethic, charity, and submission to the standards of a transcendent realm.[11] With changes in Christianity and Judaism and the infusion of new religions from around the world, we have become a somewhat different nation, more vulnerable to the tendencies Tocqueville warned us against.

As much as we individualistically strive for wealth to purchase or find what is new, we affirm our equality with others.[12] In fact, we are so proud of our equality that we resent those who claim to be above us.

There is in fact a manly and legitimate passion for equality that incites men to want all to be strong and esteemed. This passion tends to elevate the small to the rank of the great; but one also encounters a depraved taste for equality in the human heart that brings the weak to want to draw the strong to their level and that reduces men to preferring equality in servitude to inequality in freedom.[13]

Thus, Tocqueville posed the question of how we Americans can reconcile our love for equality with our regard for liberty and excellence.

For a book on California politics, so far we have spoken little of California and perhaps even less on politics. But these Tocquevillean insights are essential for understanding our current political condition. After all, the United States is a democratic republic that depends, more than any other form of government, on the character of its citizens to be successful.[14] There can be no politics without citizens. What sorts of citizens are indifferent to politics, obsessed by the pursuit of wealth, isolated from each other, insistent on novelty, and attached to one's equality with each other—perhaps more attached to this than to excellence, especially if greater freedom is perceived in another? Tocqueville's principal goal was to fight the penchants or inclinations that turn us away from a life of active citizenship.

Now, all this is not a complete portrayal of the Californian or of the American. We have omitted, for now, what Tocqueville would have noted about the self-sacrifice of Americans in bloody wars and in modest charity; the rich network of associations ranging from the Boy Scouts to civic groups; and, above all, the vital role of religion in shaping the American character. Tocqueville sought to counter the undesirable facets of the American character with the admirable ones. We are today even more American in many regards that Tocqueville noted. California politics has been decisively shaped by these and other attitudes, and we cannot understand democracy in California unless we consider them and their consequences. *Democracy in California* seeks to consider these in order to foster the spirit of citizenship. We do so through understanding how our democratic character, as portrayed by Tocqueville, has shaped the growth of our political institutions and how those institutions function today. Thus, to paraphrase Tocqueville, in California we see more than California.

The recall of Governor Gray Davis of October 7, 2003, reaffirmed Tocqueville's notion of the sovereignty of the people and its peculiar California interpretation. But even more it vindicates the authors' unique emphasis on the Progressive political theory of California democracy emphasized throughout the earlier editions. With the recall of Governor Davis, the election of action movie star Arnold Schwarzenegger as governor, and his two-term governorship we have seen much Progressive theory put into actual practice. This new edition of *Democracy in California* takes into consideration the second installment of the governorship of Jerry Brown, updates vital information, and corrects some errors in the previous text.

For a more comprehensive, in-depth study of California politics and policies, now thrust forward on a national if not a world stage, readers may wish to revisit a collection of readings, assembled by the authors, *The California Republic: Institutions, Statesmanship, and Policies* (Rowman & Littlefield, 2004).[15] The collection contains both long, scholarly essays and briefer policy analyses. All strive to bring forth elements of the California political character neglected by other books. The contributions will engage both the beginning student and the scholar of California politics.

1

Diversity

Beyond the frontiers of the Union toward Mexico extend vast provinces that still lack inhabitants. The men of the United States will penetrate into these solitudes even before those who have the right to occupy them. They will appropriate the soil, they will establish a society on it, and when the legitimate proprietor finally presents himself, he will find the desert fertilized and foreigners sitting tranquilly on his inheritance.[1]

When one finally penetrates into the new states of the Southwest, where the social body, formed yesterday, still presents nothing but an agglomeration of adventurers or speculators, one is confounded to see into whose hands public power is placed, and one wonders by what force, independent of legislators and of men, the state can grow and society prosper there. . . . There are certain laws whose nature is democratic and which nonetheless succeed in part in correcting these dangerous instincts of democracy.[2]

TOCQUEVILLE WAS WRITING ABOUT what we know today as Louisiana (which achieved statehood in 1812), Mississippi (1817), and Alabama (1819), followed by Arkansas (1836). Western governments attracted an unsavory set of characters—and the early history of California has certainly borne that out. Reform of the early legislatures became the principal work of the later ones, in an attempt to root out or at least suppress "adventurers" and "speculators."

Like other Americans who moved west, Californians, too, were willing to adopt different ways as they sought wealth, fled debts, and savored a new way of life. Once they arrived in California, diverse ways of producing wealth created contrasting characters among them. For example, in the Central Valley, which spans inland California from Bakersfield to Stockton:

> As an agrarian culture, our hard work permeated everywhere, encompassed everyone. . . . I used to see very few cobblestone streets, cappuccino bars, or neighborhood theaters in any of our small [San Joaquin] Valley towns. Instead, the Valley's attraction was always and only its bustle of hardworking agrarian peers, and the bounty that grew out of their endless and uncomplaining work. For all our Valley boosterism, let us confess that there is little tradition of great universities, renowned symphonies, impressive museums, or enclaves of artists between Fresno and Bakersfield. Let us, then, live or die with our strength, which is the wonderful soil, the monotonous climate, and the agricultural genius and good sense of our people, a folk like none other on this planet and whose toil created an oasis.[3]

Hanson bemoans the loss of farms and the character they instill. As historian Kevin Starr wrote, Los Angeles and Southern California represent something else: "Dreams have a way of struggling towards materialization. Los Angeles did not just happen or arise out of existing circumstances, a harbor, a river, a railroad terminus. Los Angeles envisioned itself, then materialized that vision through sheer force of will. Los Angeles sprung from a Platonic conception of itself, the Great Gatsby of American cities."[4]

Finally, the essayist Richard Rodriguez has speculated on San Francisco's meaning:

> For most of its brief life, San Francisco has entertained an idea of itself as heaven on earth, whether as Gold Town or City Beautiful or the Haight-Ashbury.
>
> San Francisco can support both comic and tragic conclusions because the city is geographically *in extremis*, a metaphor for the farthest-flung possibility, a metaphor for the end of the line, Land's End.
>
> But the metaphor may mislead, and to understand California we may need to supply yet other perspectives, not excluding our own, at least as a start:
>
> To speak of San Francisco as land's end is to read the map from one direction only—as Europeans would read it or as the East Coast has always read. In my lifetime San Francisco has become an Asian city. To speak, therefore, of San Francisco as land's end is to betray parochialism. My parents came here from Mexico. They saw San Francisco as the North. The West was not west for them. They did not share the Eastern traveler's sense of running before the past—the darkening time zone, the lowering curtain.[5]

To think of California in this way is to appreciate both the extremism and the moderation of the Golden State—in a word, its reflection of the American character itself.

Southern California tended to be settled by southerners, northern California by northerners (as evidenced by the use of the Iowa and New York constitutions as models for the first California constitution). Great men rose to the challenges posed by Californians' needs, which included that most basic need of water: "Working in their special medium, imagined public works, the early water engineers of California were artists and prophets of social and moral development. Prophesying the bringing of water to the desert and to the cities on the plain, they saw themselves embarked upon a work of social redemption Biblical in metaphor and suggestion."[6]

California was a tangible product of the imagination. California represents an incredible diversity of ways of life, attracting streams of people from around the country and world. Unlike many states, California is not restricted to a few sources of wealth. Its natural and technological resources include aerospace, agriculture (the most diversified in the world), oil and natural gas, real estate, Silicon Valley, and entertainment, and all industries are amplified by export to the rest of the United States and the entire world. World trading partners include the People's Republic of China, Mexico, and Europe. California Overseas Trade and Investment Offices are found in major world cities, including London, Tokyo, Jerusalem, and Johannesburg.[7]

What does all this diversity mean? As Richard Rodriguez puts it, "Diversity admits everything; stands for nothing."[8] But clearly its most contentious contemporary meaning is political and refers to differences based on race, ethnicity, and gender, and how we should take account of these differences.

Out of a geographically and ethnically diverse collection of inhabitants, drawn to California for different reasons, how do we get one state of citizens? Can there be one nation if ethnic groups look upon others as "they" or even as "the Americans"?[9] How does California prepare its people to be American citizens? The challenges to a common citizenship exist not only geographically—witness the recent proposal for the separation of California into six states—but ethnically as well.[10]

The United States was unified through both necessary and noble means—that is, by appealing to the common and the high in human nature.[11] First, one must note the effects described by James Madison in *The Federalist* (no. 10, 1787), of a people bound together by a modern economy, which encourages a diversity of means of employment. Class conflict is minimized as people identify themselves with different livelihoods, as well as with their locality or region, which can in turn be absorbed within a national economy. Political unity is fostered by, and fosters, this prepolitical unity based on the mutual satisfaction of needs.[12] As Americans have known from George Washington's farewell address, such economic exchange—such as manufactured goods for agricultural ones—produces national unity in its most elementary form.[13] But full political unity required a bloody civil war. As interpreted by Abraham Lincoln, this war was necessary to affirm the fundamental proposition that justifies the nation's institutions and existence: the self-evident truth of human equality.[14] The nobility and the cosmic significance of this struggle are explicated in Lincoln's Gettysburg Address. Equality means that each and every individual has certain inalienable rights, including the rights to life, liberty, and the pursuit of happiness. Government must proceed via the consent of all, and thus is by nature limited. This is what the founders of America sought to establish nationwide, and each state was expected to imitate these general principles of republican government.

What makes any political community one body? A political community is not simply a pact for the mutual exchange of goods and services. For human beings to become common citizens, they must see beyond their families and their tribes (or nationalities). They must see each other as more than trading partners. In traditional families there is a clear hierarchy: Tribes regard each other with suspicion, as if not sharing a common humanity. Among citizens, as Aristotle (384–322 BCE) indicates, men and women must regard each other as equals. Aristotle struggles with this key political question of citizenship throughout the *Politics*.[15] His conclusion is that citizens must see themselves as members of a single regime, or constitutional order, that serves the common good—in other words, as citizens. Citizens both obey and rule, and they are better citizens and better men and women for doing so. Abraham Lincoln illustrated the psychology of citizenship in a pre–Civil War speech:

> The man of the highest moral cultivation, in spite of all which abstract principles can do, likes him whom he *does* know, much better than him whom he does *not* know. To correct the evils, great and small, which spring from want of sympathy, and from positive enmity, among *strangers,* as nations, or as individuals, is one of the highest functions of civilization.[16]

Thus, Lincoln combined the wisdom of Aristotle with that of the Founding Fathers. How can a California full of strangers, full of people who by occupation and prejudice oppose and may even oppress each other's interests, become a people of a single citizenship? After all, in a globalized economy one might feel a kinship more to the land of one's trading partners or ancestors than to where one actually lives. As Aristotle taught, the unity of a nation rests on its constitution, laws, and citizens. Let us see how Californians sought to create this unity from the diverse elements of the Golden State. In other words, the study of diversity leads to the study of California's constitution and citizenship.

The study of constitutional government in California reveals a development of principles rooted in its last constitutional convention, which was held in 1878–1879. Although California has changed since then, our constitution and major political developments grew from patterns formed by the constitution of 1879. As much as we may hate to admit it, we Californians are who we are—as human beings in our profoundest and most superficial ways, as citizens with our political passions and passivity—on account of our collective past, regardless of when we or our ancestors arrived in the Golden State.

We can study state government as an example of American constitutional principles at work. In the case of California, we can see what happens to a government that lacks the means of securing the rights that the founders gave America in the Declaration of Independence and the Constitution. In sum, California constitutional history shows us, in the growth of Progressivism, a justification for politics based on the satisfaction of passions, whether for wealth, status, recognition, or power of whatever kind. There has been a gradual substitution of will for reason and mounting tensions between majoritarian impulse and genuine deliberation. As California government increasingly becomes the instrument for gratifying citizens' needs, these dynamics produce the centralized government Tocqueville feared. With the need for government at both the state and national levels, state governments would eventually become instruments of the national one. The development of California government provides wonderful examples of the American character that we sketched in our previous chapter: apolitical, obsessed with wealth, taken with novelty, and jealous of equality with others.

With this in mind, we reconsider the fabled Gold Rush of 1848. One historian calls the Gold Rush "the most significant event in the first half of the nineteenth century. . . . No other series of events produced so much movement among peoples; called into question so many basic values—marriage, family, work, wealth, and leisure."[17] The Argonauts, as prospectors were called (after the classic Greek heroes who sought the Golden Fleece), could find instant riches similar to winning the lottery or investing cleverly in the stock market today, but the risky endeavor often entailed leaving behind an anxious family, outraged creditors, or scoffing neighbors. Many struck it rich by hitting pay dirt, but for others the ruinous venture did not pan out. Observers as early as Sir James Bryce, in his classic *The American Commonwealth* (first published 1886, revised through 1912), reflected on the similarity between mining and gambling and their effects on the California character:

The chief occupation of the first generation of Californians was mining, an industry which is like gambling in its influence on the character, with its sudden alternations of wealth and poverty, its long hours of painful toil relieved by bouts of drinking and merriment, its life in a crowd of men who have come together from the four winds of heaven, and will scatter again as soon as some are enriched and others ruined, or the gold in the gulch is exhausted.[18]

Surely Gold Rush California is this much of Tocqueville's America in a nutshell: the desire for wealth, novelty, and equality (in the sense of achieving wealth).[19]

But with the boom in California's American population, it became an immediate candidate for statehood and even bypassed territorial status. Much to the grumbling of the South, the **Compromise of 1850** admitted California as a free state, along with addressing other controversial national issues. These included prohibition of the slave trade in Washington, D.C.; territorial status for New Mexico and Utah without reference to slavery; and, most controversial of all for Northerners, stricter fugitive slave laws. California tipped the balance between free and slave states, making evident the free future of America, and thus led to the secession of the South and to the Civil War.[20] To understand what it means to be a Californian, one must understand the Civil War—a task we can only call attention to, not undertake, here.

Eagerly anticipating statehood, Californians wrote the **California Constitution of 1849**, and patterned it mostly after the Iowa Constitution but also after that of New York. The early Californians believed, as did the founders of this country, in self-government and all the risks it entailed. We hear as well echoes of the early Massachusetts Bill of Rights of 1780 in the preamble and first article of the constitution of 1849:

> We, the people of the State of California, grateful to Almighty God for our freedom, in order to secure and perpetuate its blessings, do establish this Constitution. . . . All men are by nature free and independent, and have certain inalienable rights, among which are those of enjoying and defending life and liberty; acquiring, possessing, and protecting property; and pursing and obtaining safety and happiness.[21]

Published in both English and Spanish, the first constitution provided for a limited government that protected individual rights and sought the common welfare. By contrast, the **California Constitution of 1879** would contain class struggle and anti-immigrant animus and encourage the development of the constitution into today's lengthy legal code that is twelve times the size of the U.S. Constitution.[22] As Gordon Lloyd points out, "There is a degree of public spirit, liberality, civility, and enlightenment in 1849 that is missing from subsequent discourses on the ends of constitutionalism."[23]

The original California Constitution reflected the American founders' document as much as it did the early American state constitutions. We should recall here that the genius of the American Constitution is its unique separation of powers and its dependence on federalism as a means of preserving liberty and providing for energetic yet limited government. Its theoretical principle is the inherent equality of human beings that requires limited government by consent. James Madison's *Federalist* (no. 10, 1787) argued that only a large, commercial democratic republic that fostered deliberation could effectively prevent a majority faction and thus protect the **natural rights** described in the Declaration of Independence—life, liberty, and the pursuit of happiness. In the American founders' view, the smaller the political unit, the more readily an oppressive majority could form. If any governments needed the protection of what Madison called "auxiliary precautions"—such as the separation of powers—it was the state governments. Constitutionally, California exemplifies what the founders feared in state governments and wanted to prevent at the national level.[24] How else could Jefferson's sacred principle—"that though the will of the majority is in all cases to prevail, that will to be rightful must be reasonable; that the minority possess their equal rights, which equal law must protect, and to violate would be oppression"—be preserved?[25] As for the relationship between the U.S. Constitution and the California Constitution, the latter is obviously subordinate to the former by the general principles of federalism; the former's Supremacy Clause (Article VI, section 2); and the Fourteenth Amendment, which was ratified in 1868. With the other amendments passed immediately after the Civil War, the Fourteenth Amendment was intended to bring the Constitution into conformity with the Declaration of Independence. The Tenth Amendment does, however, continue to protect a disputed realm of state powers that the federal government may not violate.

Whatever their differences on many vital issues, the American founders agreed that majority rule must follow reason, as embodied in natural rights and constitutionalism. That men and women are born with natural rights means that they have inherent freedoms that no one may violate, without their consent, as expressed in their adoption of constitutional government. These principles may be summed up in the notion that "it is the reason, alone, of the public, that ought to control and regulate the government. The passions ought to be controlled and regulated by the government."[26] To be legitimate, government must obey a rule of reason. The mere possession of power can never justify the choice of a particular policy.

After the Civil War, new conditions led to a new California Constitution. Aided by the completion of the transcontinental railroad in 1869, California's population soared from its early statehood number of 50,000 to about 865,000. No longer primarily a mining economy, the booming new state suffered dramatically from the nationwide depression of the 1870s. The Workingmen's Party blamed the railroads, corporations, and the activities of Central Pacific Railroad's "Big Four" for their miseries.[27] The Big Four were politician Leland

Stanford (1824–1893), financier Collis P. Huntington (1821–1900), foreman
Charles Crocker (1822–1888), and bookkeeper Mark Hopkins (1814–1878).

The Workingmen's Party struck out as well against the growth of **Chinese
immigration**. Known as "Celestials" after the Celestial Empire of China, California's seventy thousand or more Chinese—about 8 percent of the population—emigrated to work in the mines and railroads and then sought return
to China. In the cities they formed Chinatowns, which were associated with
vice. Keep in mind that the Chinese American population during this era was
overwhelmingly adult male and that many of the early Chinese and white
female immigrants to California were prostitutes. The constitution of 1879
reflected all these concerns—protecting the people from corrupt politicians,
preventing high rates of taxation, overthrowing the power of the corporations
(in particular the railroads), and all but expelling the Chinese by restricting
their fundamental rights. "Asiatic coolieism is a form of human slavery,"
the new constitution declared, while prohibiting employment of Chinese by
corporations and the government, discouraging immigration, and encouraging the "removal of Chinese."[28] The Chinese were seen as vice-ridden and
unscrupulous competitors with the workingmen. Irish immigrant Denis Kearney, who led a class and anti-Chinese movement, ended his speeches with
the refrain, "The Chinese must go!" Mobs attacked Chinatowns and conducted gruesome lynchings of Chinese throughout the state. The respectable
establishment of the state was appalled at the violence and sought to establish
order, but government by consent can bring only a limited amount of enlightenment, so California's last constitutional convention passed a document that
clashed with the U.S. Constitution, federal law, and international treaties. Of
course, the state's new constitution and laws had to give way. In response to
these legal assaults, the Chinese were not passive victims but fought the discriminatory legislation in courts through their own lawyers, through Chinese
counsel, and with the aid of sympathetic whites.[29] "The declaration of your
independence, and all the acts of your government, your people, and your
history, are against you," contended a Chinese immigrant's 1852 response
to the California governor's opposition to the naturalization of his fellows.[30]

Similar questions about ethnic divisions and Americanization arise today,
more than a century later. Consider Peter Skerry's reflections on the effect of
a heavily bureaucratized, ethnic-focused public policy:

> [T]his style of politics is dependent upon displays of angry protest. But mainly
> its goals are pursued through quiet bureaucratic and judicial channels, where
> the racial minority perspective has been thoroughly institutionalized by govern-
> mental and foundation elites. Transformations such as that of the Los Angeles
> County Board of Supervisors will be wrought with little opposition or notice
> from the public. . . . In essence, this approach is profoundly antipolitical. It

teaches those without political power that it can and should be bestowed on them by elite benefactors, whether Anglo or Latino. This approach also transforms Mexican-American leaders into one more voice of principled disharmony and rigidly defined abstract rights, resistant to compromise in the political arena. In the name of politics, we now have a new source of discord—of antipolitics.[31]

Thus, Skerry endorses ethnic politics but not ethnic spoils, a difficult balancing act. In his view, "being a Mexican-American in the Southwest is simply not the same as being a Pole in Chicago."[32] If one is an immigrant, the ability to return to Mexico lessens one's identity with America. Perhaps the major actor in this drama of identity is California higher education: At colleges and universities, the identity politics of race and gender emphasize the place of ethnicity in student lives to an extent that they had never previously faced. Can a person who doesn't speak Spanish be called Latino? Can an ethnic identity forgo irregular verbs? An ethnic group that spans the human range of skin, eye, and hair colors can suddenly become nonwhite, a separate race. Skerry points out the example of a Latino police officer in the notorious Rodney King beating, who was routinely described in news reports as white. Skerry also quotes a black community leader who stated that "Latinos can't make up their minds whether they're a minority."[33] Nonetheless, in the view of the media, California reached nonwhite majority status sometime in 2000.[34]

And we Californians, with the rest of America, embrace a diversity of religions—the "new religions of America."[35] For example, this is not the variety present between Protestantism and Orthodoxy, the differences between the Franciscans and the Jesuits in Catholicism, or what distinguishes the branches of Judaism. Buddhists, Hindus, Jains, Muslims, and Sikhs bring a dramatically new way of viewing the sacred—visually expressed in the architecture of their temples, mosques, and other houses of worship. Do these reinforce the American civil religion, which honors the Declaration of Independence and the Constitution and makes America a special nation, or do they transform the nation in unprecedented ways?

We should realize that this task is not simply a sentimental one. Richard Rodriguez critiques multiculturalism:

> I submit that America is not a tale for sentimentalists. . . . If I am a newcomer to your country, why teach me about my ancestors? I need to know about seventeenth-century Puritans in order to make sense of the rebellion I notice everywhere in the American city. Teach me about mad British kings so I will understand the American penchant for iconoclasm. Then teach me about cowboys and Indians; I should know that tragedies created the country that will create me.[36]

A common education should help make us one people, but sometimes what is learned, especially in one's higher education, makes this unity more difficult to achieve.[37]

Above all, we need to see the political significance of these differences. Despite the talk of a nonwhite majority in California (which is the case only if one counts all Latinos as nonwhite), 62 percent of voters in 2014 were white, 17 percent were Latino, 11 percent were Asian, another 6 percent were black (see table 1.1). The majority of voters in 2014 were from Southern California; one in five was from the Bay Area. Democrats made up the plurality of voters (44 percent). Republicans were 32 percent of voters.[38]

California political views also vary. According to the most recent publicly available data, 38 percent of voters surveyed said they were conservative, while 34 percent called themselves liberal.[39] The causes for differences in political views are diverse. They include one's experiences as a member of a racial or ethnic group, but at least as much from the region one lives in, the work one performs, and the views one forms through education. Although geographic location, occupation, race, ethnicity, and income level can all affect one's views on politics, ultimately the individual must consciously determine his or her views, through an examination of the most thoughtful views on politics.

TABLE 1.1
Demographics of Likely Voters in California, 2014

	Adult Population (%)		Likely Voters (%)	
Race/Ethnicity				
White, non-Hispanic	44		62	
Latino	34		17	
Black	6		6	
Asian	14		11	
Region				
San Francisco Bay Area	20		22	
Central Valley	17		16	
Southern California	55		52	
Los Angeles County		(27)		(25)
Orange/San Diego Counties		(17)		(18)
Inland Empire		(11)		(9)
Party I.D.				
Democrat	43*		44	
Republican	28		32	
Nonpartisan/other	29		24	

*Party I.D. population figures are percent of registered voters.

Source: Public Policy Institute of California, "California's Likely Voters," http://www.ppic.org/main/publication_show.asp?i=255 (accessed January 20, 2015).

Through laziness, ignorance, or indifference, we must not succumb to what Tocqueville called the **tyranny of the majority**, which is the inability or unwillingness to express or even think politically significant thoughts that clash with those of one's peers. "The moral empire of the majority," Tocqueville wrote, "is founded in part on the idea there is more enlightenment and wisdom in many men united than in one alone, in the number of legislators than in their choice. It is the theory of equality applied to intellects."[40] Political correctness is a form of tyranny of the majority, which is a corruption of democracy. Preserving liberty requires work, just as athletic, academic, or any other form of excellence does.

The danger of losing liberty to the forces of majority tyranny (a notion applicable to majorities of the various communities one belongs to) is particularly acute in the debate over illegal immigration. Few wish to restrict immigration altogether. Each side maintains that its position strengthens the place of liberty in American life.

Opponents of illegal immigration emphasize law-abidingness (including respect for immigrants who obey the rules) as a fundamental principle, whose defiance promotes greater lawlessness. Illegal immigrants, who are typically from lower-income, poorly educated backgrounds, burden government-run social services and education. Immigrants lower wages of native low-income workers. Thus, to speed the integration of immigrants into American society, the rate of illegal immigration must be slowed down. For security's sake alone, borders should be made secure. Americanization programs should emphasize the duties involved in citizenship (even in matters as ordinary as a driver's license) and the gratitude immigrants and citizens in general should feel.

Those who advocate what opponents call "amnesty" insist that over twelve million illegal immigrants cannot be returned and should not be threatened, without risking drastic consequences to the economy, particularly the agricultural, construction, and services sectors. Given the opportunity, this argument goes, even illegal immigrants will become part of American life, contributing to the dynamism and prosperity of a country with historically open borders, as generations of immigrants have before. The choice to immigrate already displays a principal virtue of the American character, the desire for self-improvement.

Issue Highlight for Chapter 1: Illegal Immigration

Illegal immigration evokes passionate, and seemingly contradictory, opinions. In Murrieta, California, demonstrations—for and against—the president's immigration policy received widespread news coverage.[41] This issue became even more heated after President Obama's executive order in November 2014. This order lessened the threat of deportation for undocumented parents of U.S. citizens and for those who came to the United States as children.[42] In a public opinion poll, taken shortly after the announcement of the executive order, 56 percent of Americans thought that the president's proposal should be blocked.[43] Yet, in the same poll, 62 percent of Americans favored allowing illegal immigrants, now in the United States, to have a chance to become permanent residents, if they met certain conditions. As these polls suggest, opinions about illegal immigration are complex and defy easy explanations and off-hand analyses.

Perhaps the division between and within many on the issue of immigration is reflected in the writing of Victor Davis Hanson, the scholar and vine farmer we cited at the beginning of this chapter, who lives in the farming town of Selma, near Fresno. Based on his own experience on his family farm, he has eloquently denounced the effects of illegal immigration on the quality of life for all in California. From his own observations of life around him, the deterioration stems from a growing lawlessness, the strain on government and other institutional resources, lowered education standards, and a coarsening of life. But he also acknowledges that the agricultural industry would be ruined without these workers. And Professor Hanson also notes with pride that illegal immigrant students of his have won top academic prizes and have gone on to graduate study in prestigious programs. Which problems do we want? Which riches would we deprive ourselves of? Is the real issue not that America has too many immigrants but rather not enough Americans?[44]

Conclusion

California is diverse in numerous ways, geographically and economically as well as by race and ethnicity. The Gold Rush brought about the rapid settlement of California and its entry into the Union under the Compromise of 1850. The constitutional history of California is marked by the steady growth of government under the California Constitution of 1879, which was adopted by the constitutional convention of 1878–1879 under the sway of populist and anti-Chinese demagoguery. The strident immigration debates reflect divisions over the meaning of liberty and the relationship between opportunity and obligations in American life.

2

A Progressive Constitution

Democratic peoples often hate the depositories of the central power; but they always love this power itself. . . . I have shown that equality suggests to men the thought of a lone, uniform, and strong government. I have just brought out that it gives them the taste for it; the nations of our day tend therefore toward a government of this kind. . . . I think that in the democratic centuries that are going to open up, individual independence and local liberties will always be the product of art. Centralization will be the natural government.[1]

THE GREAT NATIONAL REFORM MOVEMENT known as **Progressivism** sought to replace fundamental American political practices, such as a limited government of separated powers, with an unlimited government closer to the parliamentary model. It drew its principles from Jean-Jacques Rousseau (1712–1778) and his German followers such as G. W. F. Hegel (1770–1831), who make the will of the people the source of all legitimate rule. Because the will of the people cannot contradict itself, it cannot be limited, and hence powers should not be separated as they are in American democracy. This will is not simply a spontaneous outburst but is self-knowing and self-actualizing. Its discipline is found in the administrative state, popularly known as "the bureaucracy." The core of this European philosophy found its way into the beliefs of prominent American Progressives such as the prolific John Dewey (1859–1952). For such Americans, Progressivism stood for a scientific attitude toward politics, which explicitly rejected the natural rights basis of American politics as expressed in documents such as the Declaration of Independence. This meant that there were no inherent limits on legitimate government, as in the founding principle of just government requiring the consent of the governed. The Progressives were particularly critical of property rights–based arguments that corporate America was fond of using, so government regulation, in the name of the public interest, followed logically. Early Progressives also despised the machine politics of their era. The political machine, the spoils system, and the vibrancy of American politics received an immortal defense in the classic *Plunkitt of Tammany Hall: A Series of Very Plain Talks on Very Practical Politics*, in which George Washington Plunkitt protested that the reform movement was "underminin' the manhood of the nation and makin' the Declaration of Independence a farce."[2]

The administrative state, staffed by experts from the universities (reform politics' great ally), would take on the challenge of an industrializing society now being filled with new waves of immigrants. Progressivist politics was closely aligned with developing academic programs in the universities, especially the new discipline of political science. Evolutionary science such as the important work of Charles Darwin allegedly swept away the claims of self-evident truths of the founding generation, which rested on the notion of a knowable and enduring human nature. The will of the new political-academic elite sought to satisfy the people's security and needs.

In foreign policy, Progressivism could manifest itself in imperialism, such as American involvement in the Philippines during the Spanish-American War; in isolationism, as seen in the policies of California politician **Hiram Johnson**; or in idealist internationalism, as seen in President Woodrow Wilson (1913–1921). In California, Progressivism would adopt a hostile nativist stance, opposing Asian immigration and supporting discriminatory legislation. Contemporary liberalism certainly embodies many tenets of Progressivism, as we see in much Great Society legislation. But liberalism has also advanced a host of class-, gender-, and race-oriented domestic policy views beyond the Progressive agenda.[3]

Perhaps Progressivism's clearest signs of the reliance on an enlightened electorate are the initiative and referendum. These are means by which the electorate can directly vote in new laws or, in the case of California, amend the state constitution. (The mechanics of the initiative and referendum are discussed in chapter 5's coverage of campaigns and elections.)

In California, as well as in other states, Progressivism aimed at transforming both Democratic and Republican parties into its image of a reformed politics, one free of bosses and partisanship. For example, the Big Four's railroad dominated the economy of the state and whatever laws and judges were needed to maintain its grip.[4] Regulation of powerful industries such as railroads (although, in principle, this applied to any economic entity) was also deemed necessary to support the public interest.

Progressivism was not a labor or agriculture movement, as sprouted up in other regions of the country. It was far more a movement of middle-class respectability, born in the Midwest and with roots in New England religion.[5] Though many Progressive politicians were lawyers and journalists, many others were reform-minded businessmen who were labeled "goo-goos" for their good-government enthusiasms. Perhaps a character in Frank Norris's novel *The Octopus* best expresses the frustrations of the reformers: "California likes to be fooled. . . . Indifference to public affairs—absolute indifference, it stamps us all. Our state is the very paradise of fakirs."[6]

G. Alan Tarr summarizes Progressivism's early political achievements: "The most striking illustration of [them] . . . was the set of amendments adopted in California in 1911 that established a railroad commission to regulate all public utilities, revised the tax system to shift more of the burden to corporations and banks, and provided for employers' liability, a minimum wage, and enhanced powers of eminent domain."[7] But Progressivism's reformist, anticorporation rhetoric fueled more radical parties, even as it robbed them of adherents.

California's principal Progressive politician was Hiram Johnson, who came to prominence as a crusading attorney. He investigated the Southern Pacific Railroad and, in emotional speeches, denounced its control over the economy of the state. This "short and stocky" Republican became the dominant figure in California politics, serving continuously as governor from 1911 to 1917 and thereafter as a U.S. senator until his death in 1945.[8] He was so popular that he often captured both major parties' nominations. He was also nominated vice president for Theodore Roosevelt's Bull Moose Party in 1912, losing by a large margin to Woodrow Wilson but getting more electoral college and popular votes than Republican incumbent William Howard Taft. Johnson later sought the presidency, but this proud man would reject Harding's offer of the vice presidency on the Republican ticket in 1920.

Under Johnson's leadership, California adopted the initiative, referendum, and recall, thus injecting direct democracy into its politics. His support of **cross-filing** (the ability to capture both the Democratic and Republican nominations for the same office, as mentioned earlier), local and judicial nonpartisanship, workmen's compensation, and women's suffrage were his other notable Progressive achievements, and he envisioned other reforms.[9] As explained by John Aubrey Douglass, the Progressive reform of higher education "would provide a caste of trained labor and professionals, a source of culture and research that would build a more learned, competent, and productive society capable of wisely using these new democratic powers."[10]

Perhaps the temperamental Johnson's significance can be explained in terms of a far better-known national figure, former chief justice of the U.S. Supreme Court **Earl Warren**. Warren (1891–1974) was one of California's most renowned and controversial political figures. He served as California's attorney general (1939–1942) and thrice as its governor (1942–1953). Following his 1948 nomination for vice president, in which he ran with Republican New York governor Thomas Dewey unsuccessfully against Harry Truman and Alban Barkley, he was appointed by President Dwight Eisenhower as chief justice of the Supreme Court (1954–1969). He wrote the *Brown v. Board of Education* school desegregation decision of 1954, the reapportionment cases, and numerous other court decisions expanding civil liberties, but his most important contribution was to make the Supreme Court and other courts, federal and state, conscious political reformers. In this sense, Warren was an archetypal Progressive in his belief in active government and subsequent disdain for the separation of powers. Warren declared that he

> believed in the progressivism of Hiram Johnson, who had broken the power of the predatory interests by opening up our state and local governments so the people could govern themselves through free elections. . . . I was committed to the nonpartisanship he brought into city and county government. I believed in the civil service he established, putting an end to the spoils system of former days and enabling public employees to live without fear of discharge merely because of a change in administration. . . .
>
> I believed implicitly in the direct primary for all state and local offices, and in the cross-filing procedure for partisan state offices. These were reforms that made it possible for an impecunious young man like myself to launch on a public career that would last half a century. They sounded the death knell of the old-fashioned political boss.[11]

As we have seen, the late chief justice was fond of the practice of cross-filing. Pulitzer Prize–winning historian Don Fehrenbacher and his coauthor Norman Tutorow comment that cross-filing favored the incumbent and "also blurred party lines, undermined party responsibility, and gave California politics a peculiar cast of irrationality."[12] By favoring incumbency and implicitly giving more power to unelected elites such as new political bosses replacing the old, cross-filing aided the Progressivist cause. Such was the dominance of the Progressive Republicans that the first Democrat to capture the gubernatorial seat in the twentieth century was Cuthbert Olson, who served only one term (1939–1943).

While Progressivism flourished primarily within the Republican Party, it also had its influence on the Democrats and on radical movements. The rejection of natural rights in favor of an evolution of ever-expanding benefits would be seen in its Depression era extreme in Upton Sinclair's Eliminate Poverty in California (EPIC) movement, together with the Townsend Plan to give the elderly a monthly subsidy. Sinclair, author of *The Jungle* and a long-time socialist, surprised all observers by winning the Democratic nomination for governor in 1934. His nomination and other Depression-era measures, such as the Townsend Plan and the Ham-and-Eggs Initiative, exemplified the enduring vitality of the 1879 constitution. These radical proposals would have given the elderly scrip worth a disproportionate amount of money that had to be spent within a specific time period. Though Sinclair and his fantastic major proposals were defeated, the principle of direct majority rule that could drastically alter life remained.[13]

While they were both keen partisans, California Republican Richard Nixon and Democrat Edmund G. "Pat" Brown exhibited Progressivism as well: Nixon in his willingness to centralize the government to carry out reforms, and Brown in his expansion of the University of California system. Though a conservative, Ronald Reagan benefited from his image as a "citizen-legislator," who would come in from the outside and reform a corrupt system. Thus, he, too, made use of Progressive imagery, as did Arnold Schwarzenegger.[14]

The legacy of Progressivism remains in the California Constitution as we know it today. The constitution's sprawl is illustrated by the diversity of its contents, which combine language from the American founding era with details about state retirement benefits.[15] Amended over five hundred times since 1879, the constitution has become a complex code and a basic law for Californians. As the state's own edition of the institutions of its government puts it:

> The fundamental difference between the California Constitution and the Constitution of the United States is that the Federal Constitution is a grant of power to Congress and is also a limitation upon its powers, whereas the State Constitution is a limitation upon the power of the State Legislature. . . . The sphere of state activity is more extensive than that of the federal government since its powers are original and inherent, not derived or delegated, as are the powers of the federal government.[16]

Californians continue to live under the constitution's attempts to regulate corporate power.[17] We will discuss selected provisions of the constitution in the chapters that follow.

Reflecting the frustrations of many citizens, a 1994 Constitution Revision Commission attempted to make California government more "efficient." Dissenters protested that the commission's streamlining proposals would accelerate the Progressivist tendencies that had created the current problem of centralized administration.[18] The Progressives' intellectual arm, the universities and think tanks, has proposed more radical reforms such as a unicameral legislature, while overwhelming the separation of powers by a more consolidated executive.[19] Intended to purify politics, term limits are a Progressive measure favored by significant numbers in both parties. Party identification is prohibited for all but a few major state offices, and parties may not endorse nonpartisan candidates. The voters' natural, healthy suspicion of parties has led to the further weakening of the party system. This in turn accelerates the **centralization** that Tocqueville feared, which favors those least subject to the political process (the courts and the bureaucracy) over the elected branches and especially the bicameral legislature and local governments. The current California Constitution shows that the Progressive attacks on corrupt politics are fundamentally attacks on political activity generally. Whatever their original intent, Progressivism's practices have made it more difficult to protest the increasing reach of the administrative state that is Progressivism's hitherto highest achievement. Thus, it is far too modest for George Mowry to conclude, "The Progressive supplied an honest and decent middle way between a corrupt labor party and a corrupt corporation-dominated government."[20]

The enemies of Progressivism are as diverse as its friends, as is the case with any form of populism—once one sees the elites claiming to be the voice of the people. Whatever later mitigation of the treatment of the Chinese, the principal change had occurred—the rejection of limited government and its natural rights basis—and would continue to guide the politics of California. In the view of some, the spirit of Kearney, and not the deliberation of the earlier constitutional convention, would guide California politics. But others would defend at least instances of majoritarian governance. Though a staunch critic of unlimited democracy, Edward J. Erler contends, "It is simply to confuse form with substance to argue that . . . the people are incapable of comprehending anything but appeals to passions and prejudices."[21]

Erler is highlighting the consequences and dilemmas of Progressivism that California exemplifies and with which we still struggle today. Are Progressivism and its innovations enemies or allies of self-government? Has Progressivism itself become a house divided that might even bring itself down? Certainly critics of the initiative, referendum, and recall, such as noted journalist Peter Schrag, take this view: He maintains that these devices have fueled "the rabid antigovernment fervor of the early nineties."[22] He would point to Proposition 13, which rolled back and limited increases in property taxes; Proposition 187, which restricted illegal immigrants' rights; and Proposition 209, which prohibited race and gender preferences by state government, including public education admissions and hiring. Direct democracy is here to stay for the foreseeable future, and so will these controversies over the fundamental American principle of self-government.

Issue Highlight for Chapter 2: Affirmative Action

Proposition 209 was simple, but, as we write fifteen years later, the controversies continue to flare: "The state shall not discriminate against, or grant preferential treatment to, any individual or group on the basis of race, sex, color, ethnicity, or national origin in the operation of public employment, public education, or public contracting."[23] In November 1996, the people of California voted to make Proposition 209, the California Civil Rights Initiative, Section 31 of Article I of the California Constitution. It won by a 55–45 percent margin at the same time that Democrat Bill Clinton defeated Republican Bob Dole by a 51–38 percent margin in California. Fifty-eight percent of white women and 66 percent of white men supported Proposition 209, but three-fourths of blacks and Latinos and 61 percent of Asians opposed it.[24]

Now constitutionally deprived of preferential treatment, "underrepresented minority" enrollments at the University of California (UC), Berkeley, have fallen dramatically.[25] While enrollment of minority students has increased in the UC system overall, these numbers have not kept pace with the changing demographics of the state. Recent data suggest that the enrollment of "underrepresented minorities" in the UC system has increased from 20 to 25 percent, since the passage of Proposition 209. Yet, the percent of minority students graduating from California high schools has grown from 30 to 48 percent. The UC minority enrollment gap, therefore, has grown from 10 to 23 percent, since the passage of Proposition 209.[26] Supporters of preferences claim that affirmative action is still needed to ensure equal opportunity. Opponents claim that the constitution now vindicates the principles of equal treatment. Preferring "underrepresented" minorities harms the admission chances of Asian American applicants. All of these arguments have become more intense as California examines its higher education system and as the U.S. Supreme Court upheld Michigan's recent ban on affirmative action, which is similar to Proposition 209.[27]

Regardless of how one stands on the contentious issue of race, ethnic, and gender preferences, one wonders why representative government, with its spirit of deliberation and compromise, might not be a better means of deciding such issues, rather than up-and-down votes on ballot propositions. Yet, following Erler's argument for the use of the initiative, one might counter that some issues are of sufficiently general principle that a popular vote on them would reflect a political spirit that a democracy can ill afford to lose.

Conclusion

The 1879 constitution, which eliminated the restraints of the 1849 constitution, provided for regulation of economic life and led the way for the Progressive-era reforms of Governor (and later Senator) Hiram Johnson. On a national level, Progressivism sought to alter fundamental constitutional principles such as federalism and the separation of powers. Progressives wished

to restrain what they regarded as corrupt practices by political parties, especially when these parties favored private interests such as railroads and the
emerging corporations. Progressive reforms sought to weaken political parties and strengthen an administrative state comprised of rational, scientific
administrators. Of use in bypassing or replacing legislators are the initiative,
referendum, and recall. Republicans Hiram Johnson and Earl Warren remain
the most prominent Progressive politicians in California history. The use and
abuse of direct democracy in a diverse state will remain a controversial issue,
as reflected in the continuing debate over Proposition 209.

3

Public Opinion and the Media

The majority, being an absolute master in making the law and in overseeing its execution, having equal control over those who govern and over those who are governed, regards public officials as its passive agents and willingly deposits in them the care of serving its designs.[1]

Journalists in the United States, therefore, in general hardly have an elevated position; their education is only sketchy, and the turn of their ideas is often vulgar. . . . The spirit of the journalist in America is to attack coarsely, without preparation and without art, the passions of those whom it addresses, to set aside principles in order to grab men, to follow them into their private lives, and to lay bare their weaknesses and their vices.[2]

THE UNITED STATES IS RULED BY public opinion in the most fundamental sense. This is also true of California. With modern polling techniques, political leaders can maintain a daily vigil over the ebbs and flows of opinion. This chapter provides an explanation of the basic components of public opinion. However, the conditions for a healthy republic require something other than a voracious majoritarianism fed by the establishment media. For a republic to survive, the deliberative sense of the public must rule instead of its unfettered will.[3] We will also examine the nature of the media in state politics and how it has changed over the years.

Public Opinion

The most important measurement of public opinion occurs on election days. Voters cast ballots for individuals seeking a particular office and for initiatives, referenda, or recalls. In the interim period between elections, public opinion is most commonly measured by public opinion polls, although direct contact with voters is still important.[4] The basic components of public opinion are salience effects, attention cycles, and liberal and conservative ideologies, along with public opinion polls and their findings.

Salience Effects

There is no such thing as *a* public opinion. Public opinion is divided into various segments; its two major components are the **mass public** and the **elite public**.[5] These categories do not automatically apply to levels of income or social status, but they are determined by a person's knowledge of and interest in a particular issue. For example, consider the issue area of safety regulations for highway construction workers. A business executive who works in a high-rise office building will not necessarily be an expert on road construction and is probably just as ignorant as most other people are concerning highway construction safety. A highway construction worker, on the other hand, is quite knowledgeable about the subject. On this particular issue, therefore, a political leader might very well recognize the construction worker—with plenty of coworkers who might feel compelled to express their pleasure or displeasure at the next election—as part of the elite and the business executive as part of the mass public.

The relative interest of mass and elite publics determines the saliency of an issue. The more salient the issue, the more likely a political leader is to follow public opinion. The less salient the issue, the more likely a political leader is to interject his or her private opinions. An issue has the highest level of salience when both segments of public opinion, mass and elite, are aware of the problem and are prepared to act on their opinions. On these high-salience issues, an officeholder or candidate is under great pressure to support the position held by the majority, no matter what his or her private opinion might be. The most prominent examples of high-salience issues are taxes, the economy, and education.

Issues that rouse the elite public but not the mass public are identified as medium-salience issues. On such issues, a political leader has a difficult choice. On the one hand, the mass public has little knowledge or interest in the issue, and the political leader might see an opportunity to employ some independent judgment. On the other hand, the intensity of elite opinion might outweigh their lack of numbers. Examples of medium-salience issues include tobacco taxes, state bond issues, and public works projects.

Issues in which neither the elite nor the mass public is interested are known as low-salience issues. On such issues the officeholder or candidate has, for the most part, a free hand to take a position. Examples of low-salience issues include technical budget matters and bureaucratic reorganization. However, one must keep in mind that the salience of an issue is not the same as the importance of an issue. An issue of low salience, such as a budget item, may be extremely important and very expensive yet fail to provoke public interest.

Attention Cycles

Public interest in a particular issue is often cyclical. Political scientists refer to this phenomenon as the **attention cycle**,[6] which has three stages: The first is the crisis stage. An elected official, interest group leader, or media figure attempts to bring attention to a particular issue by labeling it as a crisis. To do this, the crisis entrepreneur will need to get the attention of the media. This is usually accomplished by a press conference at which a victim of some sort will recount his or her personal story to the press. Soon enough, there will be talk of an illegal immigration crisis, a gasoline price crisis, a living wage crisis, a traffic crisis, or a health insurance crisis.[7]

Some issues fade quickly after the crisis stage. However, a select few may gain the attention of a significant number of policymakers and make it to the second stage, legislative consideration. Such issues then become the topic of legislative hearings and gubernatorial commissions. Next, a wide variety of proposed plans leading to specific bills are introduced into the legislature.[8] The symbolic rhetoric of the crisis stage is transformed into the technical legislative language of the second stage.

Once an issue has made it into actual legislation, it enters the third and final stage. One of three things will occur: (1) the public loses interest and the crisis subsides; (2) the public comes to the opinion that the cure would be worse than the disease and the legislation dies; or (3) the issue is passed into law. The first two scenarios are the most common; rarely do issues maintain public interest long enough to become law. Very often, issues will reappear year after year, only to suffer the same fate. Elected officials are quite aware of the fickle nature of public opinion and of the need to stick to a few broad legislative goals with easily identifiable themes in order to succeed.

As we will see regarding the California legislature in chapter 6, our policy system is designed to frustrate the efforts of policymakers who rely on emotive rhetoric. The founders of this country wanted their government to reflect the careful consideration of the people, not their momentary desires. On this point, even California's progressive constitution allows for some filtering to take place. Major changes in the law are most likely to take place only if the public is willing to devote a significant amount of attention to it over an extended period of time.[9]

Conservatives and Liberals

Another common way in which public opinion is examined is by studying political ideologies.[10] The most fundamental ideological division in public opinion is that between conservatives and liberals. What do these terms mean?

The modern American conservative believes in the traditional ideas of individual freedom and responsibility. Such freedom and responsibility are not dangerous to the conservative because American conservatism, if understood properly, is derived from the idea that all human beings share an equal nature, an ability to make decisions based on a commonsense morality. This is the fundamental idea of human equality that is at the heart of the American regime. Liberalism, at its core, denies that such a commonsense morality exists and, even if such a morality were to exist, doubts the average person's ability to understand it. Therefore, a large administrative state is required to regulate even the most mundane aspects of private and public life. American conservatives take the position that they are "conserving" the traditions of the American founding. American liberalism takes the position that such traditions are restrictive, hence the need to be "liberated" from them.[11]

However, it cannot be said simply that conservatives favor less government and liberals favor more. Because the two ideologies are derived from fundamentally different views of human nature, each ideology calls for different kinds of government action in different cases. For example, a liberal is likely to be in favor of gun control but against the death penalty, while a conservative is likely to be against gun control yet in favor of the death penalty. A liberal is likely to see gun control as a necessary government restriction to prevent citizens from acting unreasonably in self-protection or otherwise. On the other hand, a liberal is likely to see the death penalty as a residual institution based on old-fashioned ideas of justice derived from moral absolutes that are irrelevant to matters of public policy.

In contrast, a conservative is likely to see the death penalty, properly administered, as an execution of a rational system of justice that is understandable to the average citizen: appropriate punishment for a particular crime. This same logic leads the conservative to be opposed to gun control; rational creatures existing in a rational world should be able to make sensible decisions regarding their own protection.

Public Opinion Polling

It is the job of the political pollster to collect accurate readings of public opinions. To do this, the pollster must undertake a scientific poll, which has two main components: an appropriate **sample** and a **stratified random distribution**.[12]

California has nearly forty million people; therefore, it would be impossible to ask every single Californian his or her opinion on a certain issue. However, a pollster can gain an estimate of the public's opinion by sampling, in which he or she takes a sample of the population, then measures the public's opinions on certain matters. When constructing a sample, the pollster's main concern is to eliminate **bias** from the sample. For example, suppose you wanted to measure the most popular baseball franchise in the state, but you only conducted a sample in San Francisco and Marin counties. Chances are that an overwhelming number of people would say the San Francisco Giants. This poll is biased to the extent that the sample is not reflective of California's overall population.

One method of eliminating bias is to select people for a sample on a random basis, such as a random selection of all the telephone numbers in the state. However, a good pollster will do more than just construct a random sample. A truly scientific sample will use a stratified random distribution so that the demographic characteristics of the sample are similar to those of the population. An unbiased sample would be one that takes a proportionate amount of people from the various regions of the state, allowing for differences in race, gender, and estimated income levels. If a stratified random distribution is used, a poll can accurately measure the nature of public opinion in California from a sample of five hundred to three thousand people.

Most public opinion polls are either phone surveys or exit polls. Phone surveys are conducted year-round, and exit polls take place only on election days. Various polling firms hire people to ask voters a series of questions as they exit the location at which they cast their ballots. Of course, participation in any survey is strictly voluntary, which may affect findings.

Recent Findings

Californians differ on a variety of issues across a number of dimensions. There can be differences of opinion on an issue according to partisanship, ideology, ethnicity, age, gender, and religion, among others. Consider the findings in table 3.1, which analyzes California public opinion on the death penalty. Overall, 56 percent of Californians favor keeping the death penalty. When looking at this issue through the lens of partisan preference, a slim ma-

TABLE 3.1
Death Penalty, California Public Opinion: approve or disapprove?

Demographic Category	Approve (%)	Disapprove (%)	No Opinion (%)
All	56	34	10
Party			
Democrats	48	43	9
Republicans	71	21	8
Nonpartisan/others	53	35	12
Ideology			
Strong Conservative	78	19	3
Moderate Conservative	72	21	7
Moderate	57	33	10
Moderate Liberal	44	45	11
Strong Liberal	29	61	10
Race/Ethnicity			
White, non-Hispanic	57	35	8
Latino	58	32	10
Black	46	42	12
Asian	47	30	13
Age			
18–29	51	39	10
30–39	61	33	6
40–49	57	33	10
50–64	61	32	7
65 or older	50	36	14
Gender			
Male	59	35	6
Female	53	34	14
Religion			
Protestant	67	23	10
Catholic	60	30	10
Non-Christian (religious)	43	49	8
No religious preference	45	48	7

Source: Field Poll, September 12, 2014, Mark DiCamillo and Mervin Field, http://www.field.com/fieldpollonline/subscribers/Rls2486.pdf (accessed January 27, 2015).

jority of Democrats support the death penalty while an overwhelming number of Republicans support it. Ideological differences offer an even sharper distinction. Among self-identified strong conservatives, support for the death penalty is 78 percent. For strong liberals, support plunges to twenty-nine percent. With respect to race and ethnicity, the differences are not as distinct. A majority of whites and Latinos support the death penalty, but there is far less support among African Americans and Asians. When breaking down opinion by age, we find that support for the death penalty is strong for those between 30 and 64, but weaker among those over 65 and those younger than 29. As for gender, there is little difference in opinion. A majority of both men and women support the death penalty. Interestingly, the percentage of men and women who *disapprove* of the death penalty is nearly identical. As for the category of religion, the strongest support for the death penalty comes from Protestants and Catholics. Sixty-seven percent of Protestants in California support the death penalty. For Catholics, the level of support is 60 percent. As for those who are not Christians yet are religious, only 43 percent support the death penalty, which is nearly identical with the amount of support—45 percent—expressed by those with no religious preference.

In table 3.2, we see an analysis of California public opinion on gun control. When a statistical sample of Californians was asked whether it was more important to have more gun control or to protect the rights of gun owners, 61 percent of Californians supported more gun control. Among Democrats, the level of support for more gun control was an overwhelming 80 percent. For Republicans, however, that figure plunges to only 31 percent. The differences between men and women on this issue are stark as well. Sixty-nine percent of women in California support more gun control but only a slim majority of men—51 percent—favor more gun restrictions.

TABLE 3.2
Gun Control, California Public Opinion: Is it more important to impose greater controls on gun ownership or protect the rights of gun owners?

Demographic Category	More Gun Control (%)	Protect Gun Rights (%)	No Opinion (%)
All	61	34	5
Party			
Democrats	80	15	5
Republicans	31	65	4
Nonpartisan/others	63	31	6
Gender			
Male	52	43	5
Female	69	26	5

Source: Field Poll, February 26, 2013, Mark DiCamillo and Mervin Field, http://www.field.com/fieldpollonline/subscribers/Rls2441.pdf (accessed January 27, 2015).

Media

The media are the primary means by which people receive political information. The media consist of television, radio, the printed press (newspapers, magazines, and newsletters), and the Internet. The media are not neutral, nor do they simply transmit information. They shape the nature of the information people receive, sometimes consciously and sometimes unconsciously.[13] However, media coverage of state and local politics is scarce. Much of the focus, even for the local press, is placed on national politics.

For most of American history, the media were organs of a particular political party. There were Democratic newspapers and Republican newspapers. The editors of the so-called partisan press would shape stories to the advantage of their favorite candidates. As methods of communication and the American public became more sophisticated, it became more difficult for newspapers to characterize events in a certain manner. As the telegraph, telephones, and radio allowed for quicker communication, people no longer had to wait for a newspaper to write, edit, and print a story. Political parties no longer felt the need to support newspapers as it became more difficult to shape public opinion through the partisan press.

To make up for this lost business, newspapers turned to sensationalism in the form of **muckraking** and **yellow journalism**. The media empire of William Randolph Hearst, headquartered in California, epitomized this change in journalism, and Hearst papers were the pioneers in these areas. Muckraking involves the exposure of corrupt practices in business and in government. Today, programs like *20/20* (ABC), *Dateline* (NBC), and *60 Minutes* (CBS) and Internet sites like *The Drudge Report* (www.drudgereport.com) are heirs to the great muckraking tradition started by Hearst. Almost every local television news broadcast in California will regularly include a muckraking story. Furthermore, newspapers and radio stations routinely feature stories of government corruption and business malpractice. Yellow journalism, on the other hand, often involves bald untruths or wild exaggerations. Yellow journalism is also known as *tabloid journalism* and is concerned with bizarre supernatural phenomena, celebrity gossip, or worldwide conspiracies.[14]

Over the past century, with the rise of professional journalism schools, the media sought to recast itself as unbiased transmitters of information. The goal of modern journalism has been to present the news with as little editorializing as possible. However, it is doubtful that the media fulfill their goal. One need only examine the editorial pages of the following newspapers and the stories selected for publication in order to determine that the political opinion of reporters does influence the type of coverage that an issue or political leader receives: consider the differences between the *Los Angeles Times*, *Orange County Register*, *San Diego Union-Tribune*, and the *San Francisco Chronicle*.

For the first half of the twentieth century, the dominant news medium was the newspaper. In the second half of the century, however, television took center stage, and network and local newscasts became the prime means of political communication. Now, as we enter a new century, newspapers and network television news are being challenged by the so-called **new media**: cable television, talk radio, and the Internet. The new media operate in a more segmented market, catering to narrow, well-defined areas of public opinion. Particular shows or websites are specifically geared to targeted audiences. The days of the general service radio or television station might be over; in fact, it is quite possible that we might be entering a new era of the partisan press.

Entertainment Industry Influence

In one sense, the influence of the entertainment industry on state politics is limited. Because the federal government has jurisdiction over the entertainment industry via the Federal Communications Commission, most of the entertainment industry's lobbying efforts focus on federal issues. On the other hand, many Hollywood stars parlay their high visibility into elected office or positions of political influence. Former governor Arnold Schwarzenegger is the prime example, but there have been others. Clint Eastwood was elected mayor of Carmel and had a prominent speaking role in the 2012 Republican National Convention. The late Sonny Bono became mayor of Palm Springs and was then elected to Congress. Actor and director Rob Reiner successfully led a drive to increase the tobacco tax in California through a ballot initiative. Finally, California's media have a large impact on national news and opinion. California hosts many of the national news and entertainment programs that shape public opinion, not only in California or the United States but also worldwide.

Issue Highlight for Chapter 3: Media Uncover Scandal

Reuben Vives and Jeff Gottlieb, two reporters for the *Los Angeles Times*, uncovered one of the most flagrant cases of local political corruption in the nation's history.[15] While examining a routine story in the city of Maywood, a small suburb of Los Angeles, the two reporters became aware that something was amiss in the neighboring city of Bell. Digging further, the reporters discovered that Bell's city manager, Robert Rizzo, was collecting an annual salary of $800,000, making him the highest paid city manager in California. In comparison, the city manager of Oakland, which has approximately twelve times as many people as Bell, made around $200,000 per year.[16] Further investigation revealed inflated salaries for several other public officials. Police chief Randy Adams had an annual salary of approximately $450,000 per year, almost twice as much as the police chief in Los Angeles. Assistant City Manager Angela Spaccia was paid about $375,000 per year. All but one of the city's council members had annual compensation packages equaling about $100,000, even though they worked a part-time schedule. A lone city council member, Lorenzo Velez, refused the exorbitant salaries that others were receiving.

When the results of the investigation were published in the *Los Angeles Times*, "Bell" became a household word across the country, synonymous with political corruption. Protesters demonstrated outside city hall. The Attorney General of California announced an investigation into public corruption in that city. The city manager, assistant city manager, police chief, and one city council member resigned, while those who refused to resign were recalled from office.[17] Furthermore, eight city officials in Bell, including the city manager, assistant city manager, mayor, and several council members, were arrested for misuse of public funds.[18] City manager Robert Rizzo was sentenced to twelve years in prison.[19] Assistant city manager Angela Spaccia was sentenced to eleven years.[20] City council member Teresa Jacobo was sentenced to two years.[21] Mayor Oscar Hernandez, council member Victor Bello, and council member George Mirabal were each sentenced to one year in jail.[22] Councilman George Cole received 180 days of home confinement.[23] Police Chief Randy Adams agreed to reimburse $200,000 to the city.[24] The impact the media have on national, state, and local politics can be quite profound. The media are an important part of our democracy. The *Los Angeles Times* was awarded a Pulitzer Prize—the highest award in American journalism—for its coverage of the Bell scandal.[25]

Conclusion

With modern polling techniques, political leaders can maintain a daily watch over the ebbs and flows of opinion on a variety of issues. However, there is no such thing as *a* public opinion. Public opinion is divided into various segments: its major division is between the mass public and the elite public. The relative interest of the mass and elite publics determines the saliency of an issue. The less salient the issue, the more likely a political leader is to interject his or her private opinion on the matter. Public interest in a particular issue takes on the characteristic of what is known as an attention cycle, and it is a rare issue that maintains public interest throughout the entirety of this cycle. The most fundamental ideological division in public opinion is that between conservatives and liberals.

The media are the primary means by which people receive political information. Media consist of television, radio, the printed press (newspapers, magazines, and newsletters), and the Internet, and these all shape the nature of the information people receive. Television, the printed press, radio stations, and websites routinely feature stories of government corruption and business malpractice. California is home to many of the national news and entertainment programs that shape public opinion not only in California or the United States but also worldwide.

4

Parties and Interest Groups

> After the freedom to act alone, the most natural to man is that of combining his efforts with the efforts of those like him and acting in common. The right of association appears to me to be almost as inalienable in its nature as individual freedom.[1]

POLITICAL PARTIES AND INTEREST GROUPS are formed by citizens who share certain opinions about government. Political parties produce candidates for public office. The association of a candidate with one party or the other—Democrat or Republican, for example—is emblematic of the candidate's opinions about government. In the best sense, political parties are the standard bearers of the principles of the American Revolution. The dominance of a particular political party over a period of time depends on its ability to restore the people's confidence in republican government.[2]

Interest groups are associations of like-minded people who attempt to influence government officials to support or oppose certain policies. Interest groups are narrower in scope than parties are; they are organized by people with specific economic or social concerns. Organizations such as a chamber of commerce, a business group, and a labor union are examples of economic interest groups. On the other hand, the National Rifle Association, an organization dedicated to protecting a person's right to own firearms, and the Million Mom March, an organization that is in favor of increased controls on firearms, are examples of social interest groups.[3]

Within the confines of state politics, there is an inverse relationship between the strength of political parties and interest groups.[4] If political parties are strong in a state, interest groups tend to be weak. If interest groups are strong, parties will be weak. The latter condition describes the nature of democracy in California.

California Political Parties

Official Definitions

Political parties, which are regulated by the State of California, are recognized and allowed to nominate candidates for state offices if they can meet at least one of two requirements.[5] The first is by means of registration: a political party will be officially recognized if the number of Californians registered in that party is equal to or greater than 1 percent of the total number of voters in the most recent gubernatorial election.[6] The total number of voters in the 2014 gubernatorial election was 7,513,972.[7] To qualify for the 2016 election by means of registration, a political party must have at least 75,140 registered voters. The second method of qualification is by means of petition. If the number of signatures on a petition is equal to or greater than 10 percent of the voters in the last general election, then the political party is considered official. Using the 2014 general election figures, a successful party petition would require 751,397 signatures. As of 2015, the officially recognized political parties in California are as follows: American Independent Party, Americans Elect Party, Democratic Party, Green Party, Libertarian Party, Peace and Freedom Party, and the Republican Party.[8] However, the Democratic and Republican parties are the two dominant parties. The remaining parties share only a fraction of the remaining registered voters.

Why Only Two Major Parties?

The Democratic and Republican parties are the two major political parties in California and in the rest of the nation. The main reason for this is the nature of our election system. Other nations, like Israel and Germany, have more than two major political parties because they employ an election system called **proportional representation (PR)**. For example, in a PR legislative election, the number of seats a party controls is determined by the percentage of the vote it receives in the election. If a party receives 10 percent of the vote, it will receive approximately 10 percent of the seats in the legislature. If it receives 60 percent of the vote, it will receive approximately 60 percent of the seats. Because it is possible to win seats in the legislature with only a small percentage of the vote, candidates have an incentive to split off and form a variety of parties.

The United States, for the most part, employs a system of **single member districts (SMDs)**. For example, in the California Legislature, representatives come from eighty districts in the assembly and forty in the senate (this will be discussed more in chapter 6 on the legislature). To have one of its candidates win a seat in these elections, a political party's candidate must win a **plurality** of votes—the most votes out of all the other candidates running for office, but not necessarily the majority—in a specific district. Under this system, candidates of a particular party could consistently receive 10 percent of the vote but *never* gain any seats in a legislature. Therefore, a serious candidate does not have an incentive to be associated with a minor party. Given the mathematical reality of the plurality requirement, it is natural that a two-party system would develop.

The more pressing question regarding the two-party system is not the explanation for its existence but whether it is just. On one side of the question, it could be said that the SMD system limits the choices of voters. Instead of being able to cast a vote for a wide variety of parties, a voter is limited, in effect, to a choice between only two candidates. This limitation could be seen as undemocratic. On the other side of the argument is the belief that a two-party system increases the stability of a regime, with stability as one of the prime requirements for a successful republic. The SMD system forces fringe elements to join one of the two major parties in order to have an effective political voice.

However, there are reasonable concerns about the political ossification that can occur with a two-party system. When the two major parties fail to understand and deal with the pressing crises of the day, the health of the regime is in jeopardy. In such situations, the fate of the country might depend on the rise of a **third party**, but because of the SMD system, three parties cannot coexist for any length of time. To survive, the upstart party must become one of the two major parties, while one of the existing major parties must fade away.

This very phenomenon occurred before in American history. During the 1830s and the 1840s, the two major political parties in the United States were the Democrats and the Whigs. By the 1850s, the failure of each to adequately address the question of slavery led to the rise of a new party. The rise of this new party caused the Whig Party to disappear, and this new party replaced the Democratic Party as the dominant American political party for the next seventy years. This upstart political party was the Republican Party.

Party Structure

Each of the political parties in California has the same basic structure. The most basic level of organization is the county central committee, for which voters directly elect members. The next level of organization is the state central committee, and its members are selected in a variety of ways: from the county committees, from party candidates for office, and from representatives from various clubs or organizations associated with each party. In addition to these organizations, there is a state chair for each political party who is elected by the state committee of each party.

Other important members of California political parties include each party's delegates to the national conventions and each party's representatives for the national party committees. Official party organizations, on the whole, are less powerful than they were a century ago because the party has very little control over the selection of candidates and, therefore, the policy proposals that those candidates espouse. Today, the most important leaders of a party are the officeholders affiliated with it.

Weakened Parties

Political parties in the United States are, for the most part, weak. A condition of weakness is defined by a party's inability to affect which candidates will hold office, the policies they propose once in office, and the selection of those who serve in the government bureaucracy. This weakness is the legacy of the Progressive movement, which became a major political force in the 1880s. Prior to this time, political party organizations could control which candidates would represent their party in the general elections. If a candidate won the general election and failed to follow the policy opinions of party leaders, they could be removed from the party's slot in the next general election. Therefore, officeholders would be wise to accommodate the leaders of their party organizations if they wanted to maintain their positions. In addition, elected officials—especially mayors and governors—had the responsibility for directly hiring people to fill government positions. A mayor, governor, or other elected official wanting to maintain good standing with a party would be sure to hire government employees who had been approved by the party organization.

Today, almost none of this occurs. Political party organizations cannot select nominees in a general election, for that selection is left to the voters in primary elections. Furthermore, elected officials have almost no control over government employment. While they are allowed to hire a few close associates as advisors, nearly all government employees are hired by means of the civil service system, whereby government jobs are given to people on the basis of merit rather than by party affiliation. Thus, the party organization has very little control over substantive government actions. In addition, local and judicial elections in California are nonpartisan; candidates are not allowed to advertise their party affiliation on the ballot.

The particular weakness of California parties can be traced to Governor Hiram Johnson (1911–1917). As detailed earlier in the text, Johnson was elected on a platform of eliminating the corrupt practices of political machines. He believed that corruption, and therefore bad government, would be eliminated by bringing the process into the open by means of a civil service and primary elections.

Governor Johnson sought to eliminate political parties as electoral institutions through the practice of cross-filing. Candidates for office could qualify as a nominee for either or *both* political parties, and political parties were prohibited from endorsing candidates in their own primary. If a candidate could win the nomination of both political parties, which often happened, the general election would be a *fait accompli*. There is no weaker condition for a political party than to be unable to prevent members of the opposite party from representing it in the general election. Although cross-filing ended in 1959, the party structure in California has never fully recovered.[9]

Why, then, do we pay any attention to California political parties? The answer is that while the organization of the party is weak, the identification by candidates with one party or the other is still meaningful. Democratic candidates tend to take different positions on issues than Republican candidates, and they also tend to act on those different policy opinions once they are in office.[10] Examples of major issues on which the two parties significantly disagree are abortion, conservation, crime, gun rights, illegal immigration, and taxation. Democrats are more inclined to be pro-choice, favor stringent environmental regulation, be less likely to favor tough anticrime measures, oppose gun rights, be less concerned about illegal immigration, and oppose tax cuts. Republicans are generally the opposite.

Relative Strength of the Two Parties

The Democratic Party has been the strongest political party in California since the 1950s. Democrats have had a clear advantage in terms of the percentage of registered voters, which explains their relative dominance in the assembly and senate. From 1954 to 2014, the Republicans won control of the senate in only two elections and won the assembly in only four elections.

However, the scope of Democratic dominance declined after 1982. Amid the national influence of Ronald Reagan during the 1980s, Republican registration increased substantially as Democratic registration dipped to below 50 percent. This partially accounts for a string of Republican victories in gubernatorial elections: three of the last five governors have been Republican. However, the elections of 2014 may signal a resurgence of the Democrat Party. Democrat Jerry Brown was reelected as governor. Democrats retained control of both chambers of the legislature and swept all statewide offices. What is remarkable about the performance of California Democrats in the 2014 election is that it took place in a year that, in many other parts of the country, was a banner one for Republicans.

Interest Groups

Interest groups are associations of like-minded people who attempt to influence government officials to support or oppose certain policies. The nature and activity of interest groups has been a matter of debate since the founding of our nation.[11] Some argue that interest groups are merely the tools of the elite, while others argue that interest groups are the means by which all segments of society make their opinions known to officeholders.[12] In fact, it is quite possible that interest groups emerge as certain elements of society become dominant, counterbalancing this larger force in order to create equilibrium.[13] However, it is also possible that people join interest groups to get material benefits—such as health plans, merchandise discounts, and magazines—or are automatically affiliated with an interest group simply because they are employed in a certain profession, such as those involved with labor unions, trade groups, and professional associations.[14]

Regulation of Interest Groups

Interest groups in California are not ad hoc organizations that gather from time to time when the need arises. To contact officeholders and attempt to influence policy, they must register with the State of California. This has been a requirement since 1893, when laws were passed to limit the political influence of the Southern Pacific Railroad, which at that time was the state's most powerful interest group. Interest groups must also file periodic statements concerning their expenses and campaign finance activities. California passed even more stringent regulations in 1949, in response to the controversial activities of Artie Samish, a powerful Sacramento lobbyist. The most recent major piece of legislation to limit the activities of interest groups was the Political Reform Act of 1974. Under this act, the Political Reform Division was created and placed under the authority of the secretary of state.[15]

Interest Group Activities

There are three main interest group activities: direct lobbying, grassroots activity, and campaign finance. *Direct lobbying* involves direct contact between an agent of an interest group and an officeholder, usually a legislator.

They are called lobbyists because it has been the tradition that interest group members attempt to speak with legislators in the lobby of the legislature as they are coming to or going from a floor session. A lobbyist is usually hired by an interest group to communicate with officeholders and express the concerns that members of an interest group might have with a particular bill. Most often, a lobbyist attempts to influence a legislator by supplying information that can prove quite useful to a legislator. California legislators must consider hundreds of bills in a two-year legislative period, and it is difficult to make decisions as to which to support and which to oppose. A lobbyist who gains a reputation for supplying a legislator with good information can be a real asset to a legislator as well as to his or her respective group.

Grassroots activity defines any actions by large groups of people and can range from phone calls to protest marches. Unlike lobbying, which involves carefully hired representatives, grassroots activity is the vehicle of the masses. However, this does not mean that it is less effective; in fact, it can be more powerful than lobbying. A well-timed avalanche of calls, emails, faxes, and letters to a legislator's office can have an instantaneous effect on whether a legislator will support or oppose a bill. What the mass of citizens may lack in expertise, they more than compensate for in sheer numbers.[16] Furthermore, grassroots activity is often initiated by organizations with professional full-time staff who can advise citizens on how to take effective action.

The final category of interest group activity is *campaign finance*. Interest groups make donations to various candidates. Some donate to officeholders, hoping to influence their vote. Others donate to officeholders as a reward for past votes. There is some evidence to suggest, however, that interest groups tend to give money to officeholders who already agree with them.[17] In this way, campaign finance is one more way that people help their allies and attempt to defeat their enemies.

Lobbying Expenditures

One should not conclude that one issue is more important than another because its interest groups spend more than other issues' interest groups do. Quite often, a large amount of spending means that during a particular legislative session, a specific category was more controversial than others. No one would seriously argue that agriculture is unimportant in California politics, but its interest groups have relatively minor expenses. This could be an indication that, compared with other issues, agriculture is not as controversial in state government circles.

The Fair Political Practices Commission, a government organization that keeps track of lobbying activity, identified the top fifteen lobbying groups between 2000 and 2010.[18] Lobbyists representing public employee unions were the top category, spending $319.32 million to influence government officials. The next largest category was business and industry groups at $254.36 million. Indian gaming groups came in third with $201.98 million in spending. Energy interests spent $182.53 million on lobbying efforts, while the health industry rounded out the top group with $43.28 million to influence policymakers.

When disaggregated into individual expenditures by specific organizations, the top five groups consist of two public employee unions, one business and industry group, and two Indian gaming groups. The California Teachers Association is the top spender at $211.85 million. The next highest group is the California State Council of Service Employees, which spent $107.47 million. The Pharmaceutical Research and Manufacturers of America came in third on the list, with $104.91 million in lobbying expenditures. Rounding out the top five are the Morongo Band of Mission Indians and the Pechanga Band of Luiseño Indians, who spent $83.60 million and $69.30 million, respectively.

Interest Groups as Factions

In *The Federalist* (no. 10), James Madison argued that one of the strengths of the new continental American republic, as opposed to the classical *polis*, would be in its having many factions as opposed to a few. Madison argued that the existence of only two or three factions within a small territory would lead to the creation of a majority faction, which would use its power to tyrannize over the minority factions. In America, with its size and scope, there is less of a chance that a majority faction would develop. No single interest is so large that it can act alone without cooperation from others. Therefore, interests are forced to compromise with one another.

The same could be said of California. The energy industry is not so large that it could not be defeated, in a political contest, by a coordinated effort of other interests. The same could be said for any number of coalitions formed by interests in California. However, one must not take away from Madison's discussion the idea that it is the competition alone that guarantees the survival of the republic. Madison advocated a commercial republic of many "factions," so that an otherwise decent nation such as the United States would have the best chance to survive.

Issue Highlight Chapter 4: Public Employee Unions

Labor unions negotiate with employers for the wages, benefits, and rules under which union members work. Union membership in the United States peaked in 1954, at 35 percent of all wage and salary employees.[19] In 2014, only

11.1 percent of the workers were union members. This decline, however, has been primarily in the private sector. While the percent of all public employees who are unionized has remained steady—at around 35 percent since the 1970s—the percent of all private employees that are unionized now stands at only 7.4 percent. Public employee union members now represent a majority of all union members. As of 2014, there were 7.9 million public employee union members, compared to 7.4 million private sector union members.[20] As an interest group, public sector employee unions have eclipsed those in the private sector. The quintessential union member is no longer a hard-hat-wearing worker in an industrial occupation. The typical union member today is a bureaucrat, professional, or service worker who is employed by a local, state, or federal government agency.

The Great Recession (2007–2009)—along with the tepid recovery—put public unions under pressure. As the economy lagged, tax receipts failed to keep up with government spending obligations. The wages and benefits that public employee unions had negotiated for their members came under more intense scrutiny. Nineteen states passed laws that reduced the powers of public employee unions.[21] In California, on the other hand, the power of public employee unions remains strong. A ballot proposition to restrict the use of union dues for political purposes was resoundingly defeated, 57 to 43 percent. For the time being, public unions in the Golden State have stymied the efforts of would-be reformers.

The next budget crisis, however, will likely bring a new round of proposals to restrict public union activities. This is due, in large part, to the peculiar position that public employee unions have in relation to employers. Unlike those in the private sector, public employee unions have a role in selecting the employers with which they will negotiate. Since the people with whom they would negotiate are officials who must stand for elections, public employee unions can influence the contracts they might receive by the ballots they cast for those officials. Elected officials risk defeat if they negotiate tough contracts with public employee union members. Such efforts by politicians would likely be met with accusations of insensitivity toward such public servants as teachers, police, and firefighters. How do we balance the need for healthy government budgets with the natural tendency of those in a democracy to organize in the pursuit of their interests?

Conclusion

Political parties and interest groups are formed by citizens who share certain opinions about the nature of government. Political parties produce candidates for election to public office. Members of political parties tend to share a broad set of ideas concerning the nature of government. If political parties are strong in a state, interest groups will be weak; if interest groups are strong, parties will be weak. The Democratic and Republican parties are the two major political parties in California. California has two major political parties because, like the rest of the nation, it employs an SMD election system. Despite political party weakness in California, the identification of a candidate with one party or the other conveys important information to the voter. Interest groups, which are narrower in scope than political parties, are associations of like-minded people who attempt to influence government officials to support or oppose certain policies. There are three main categories of interest group activity: direct lobbying, grassroots activity, and campaign finance.

5

Campaigns and Elections

If passing events sometimes succeed in combating the passions of democracy, enlightenment, and above all mores, exert a no less powerful, and more lasting, influence on its penchants.[1]

ELECTIONS ARE THE VITAL LINK between the citizen and the government in a republic. State and local elections afford a citizen the chance to decide matters that are closest to home. This link can be direct or indirect. In *representative democracy*, citizens may vote for people they trust to make decisions on whether or not to support certain issues. In *direct democracy*, citizens have the opportunity to vote on issues themselves, without any mediation from representatives.

The American Founders were wary of direct democracy and for good reason.[2] Until the time of the American founding, human experiments with democracy had often been disastrous. Democracy had a tendency to degenerate into anarchy or tyranny, and almost all of these early democracies had been direct democracies. The Founders rescued the reputation of democracy by creating representative institutions in which people could place trusted agents in office to act on their behalf. These agents would gather together in an environment of deliberation and debate to carry out these actions.

While a representative democracy does not guarantee that wise decisions emerge, the Founders thought that it would give the reason of the public the best chance to flourish. The prevalence of direct democracy at the state level of government, and particularly in California, poses significant questions about the understanding of democracy bequeathed to us by the Founders. Can a system of direct democracy coexist with a representative democracy and provide a result that enables us to maintain "life, liberty, and the pursuit of happiness"?[3]

All Elections Are State Elections

The legacy of American *federalism* is that, in a sense, all elections are state elections. Elections for the presidency, Congress, governorship, state legislature, state judiciary, and local offices are conducted by the states. A federal system is one in which sovereignty is shared between the national and state governments. For example, we do not elect a president by popular vote in a single national election.[4] Presidents are elected by means of the Electoral College, by which a separate election occurs within each state.[5] Furthermore, members of Congress—senators and representatives—are elected as residents of a particular state, not as national citizens. The focus of this chapter will be on elections for officers who will preside over California government: the governor, elected executives, legislators, judges, and local officials.

Voter Qualifications

The chief elections officer in California is the secretary of state, who is responsible for the enforcement of candidate eligibility requirements, maintenance of registration rolls, distribution of ballots, and the overall integrity of California elections. The secretary of state is assisted at the local level by county clerks or county registrars of voters.

A person is eligible to vote in an election if he or she has reached eighteen years of age by election day, is a U.S. citizen, is an official resident of California, is not a felon serving a sentence in prison or on parole, and has not been found by a court to be mentally incompetent to register and vote. In addition, a person must register to vote at least fifteen days before an election.

Mail Ballots

Mail ballots are supplied to any California voter on request. The voter completes this ballot and mails it to the appropriate county official or returns it in person by the close of the polls on election day. These ballots are not opened or counted until election day. The original idea behind mail ballots was to provide an opportunity to vote for those who would be *absent* from the jurisdiction at the time of the election, but now any eligible voter in California may request an absentee ballot.

Candidate Qualifications

All candidates must be registered voters. Other eligibility requirements vary with the office being sought. For all state-level offices—executive and legislative—no person that has been convicted of a felony involving public funds can run for election. Some elected statewide executives must meet all those requirements, in addition to a specific requirement for that particular office. Candidates for governor and lieutenant governor must be U.S. citizens. Candidates for attorney general must have been admitted to practice before the California Supreme Court for at least five years. Candidates for insurance commissioner must relinquish any business interests in the insurance industry, if they are elected to office.[6] Candidates for the state senate, state assembly, and local offices, must live in the jurisdiction that they seek to represent. Requirements for judicial offices will be discussed in chapter 8.

Types of Elections

Elections occur in California several times a year. State and local elections each have their own schedule. Elections for governor and the other directly elected executives occur every four years and take place in even-numbered, nonpresidential years (e.g., 2010, 2014, and 2018). State assembly members have two-year terms and stand for reelection in even-numbered years. Senators have four-year terms, with only half of the senate up for reelection every two years: those from even-numbered districts stand for election in the same years in which the governor is up for election, and those from odd-numbered districts stand for election in presidential election years. Judicial elections have their own special characteristics. The years in which elections for local offices take place vary with each locality, and many local elections take place in odd-numbered years.

Partisan and Nonpartisan Elections

Candidates for most elected executive offices and for the legislature compete in **partisan elections**, in which candidates for these offices may run as representatives of political parties. Political party identification conveys to the voter a general impression of the opinions and potential actions of the candidates. Democratic candidates generally have different views about the proper role of government than Republican candidates. Candidates for the superintendent of public instruction, the state judiciary, and all local offices run in **nonpartisan elections**, in which candidates are not allowed to run as official representatives of a particular party.

The idea behind nonpartisan elections is that certain functions of government—education, the law, and local matters—are not appropriate subjects of partisan debate. However, what is partisanship but the organization of people around particular ideas about the appropriate role of government, including education, the law, and local matters? Elected officials in nonpartisan offices cannot leave their opinions about these matters at the office door. The conduct of their job requires specific opinions and solutions for certain problems.

Primary Elections

Whether partisan or nonpartisan, there are two main types of elections for offices in California: **primary elections** and **general elections**. A partisan primary election is used to determine which candidates will represent each party in the general election, and a nonpartisan primary is used to winnow the field down to an eventual officeholder. The winner of a general election attains the office under consideration.

In a typical nonpartisan primary—a city council seat, for example—several candidates seek to hold the office. If any candidate receives a majority of the vote, then that candidate is awarded the office. If, however, no candidate receives a majority, the general election will take place between the two candidates receiving the most votes in the primary.

A partisan primary is different. In most of these primary elections, several candidates from each party face off against one another for the privilege of representing their party in the general election for that office. The people with the most votes from each party will face one another in the general election. However, it is often the case that an **incumbent**—a person who already holds the office and is running for reelection—will not face any primary challengers and will automatically move on to the general election. Political parties generally discourage primary challenges to incumbent candidates for fear that a strong primary challenge will leave the candidate with less money and energy for the general election campaign, a race in which the candidate could lose the office to the other party.

Types of Partisan Primaries

Five main types of primaries have been employed in the United States: closed, open, runoff, blanket, and "top two." Each state has the responsibility to determine which method will be used. A *closed primary* is one in which only registered members of a particular party may vote; only registered Democrats are allowed to select Democratic candidates, only registered Republicans are allowed to select Republican candidates, and so forth. An *open primary* is one in which voters may participate in a party's primary without having to register with the party. A *runoff primary* is similar to a nonpartisan primary. All candidates, regardless of party, appear on the same ballot. If any candidate receives a majority of the vote, they are awarded the office. If no candidate achieves a majority, then the top two candidates from the primary election face off in the general election. In a runoff primary, it is possible that the two candidates in the general election could be from the same party. The fourth type is known as a *blanket primary*. The blanket primary was used in California from 1998 to 2000 before being declared unconstitutional by the U.S. Supreme Court.[7] It is a hybrid of the open and runoff primaries. A voter can participate in a blanket primary without having to register for any party. In a blanket primary, all of the candidates for a particular office—regardless of party—appear on the same ballot. A voter may decide to select a Republican candidate for governor, a Democratic candidate for lieutenant governor, a Libertarian for attorney general, and so on. After the votes are counted, the top candidates from each party square off in the general election. Finally, the last of the major primary types of partisan primaries is the *top two primary*. This type of primary was instituted in 2011 as a result of Proposition 14, which passed in 2010.[8] It is similar to the runoff primary. All candidates for office run on the same primary ballot, regardless of party. In addition, candidates have the option of refusing to identify a party preference, when appearing on the ballot. Unlike a runoff primary, in which a candidate could win a seat outright with a majority, the top two candidates would progress to the general election, even if the top vote-getter won a majority of the primary vote. As is the case in a runoff primary, it is possible for the top two candidates to be from the same political party. The top two primary applies to elections for statewide offices, state senate, state assembly, U.S. Senate, and U.S. House of Representatives.

Primary elections for statewide offices take place on the first Tuesday after the first Monday in June. These elections take place in even-numbered, non-presidential-election years. General elections for statewide offices take place on the first Tuesday after the first Monday in November of the election year. Primary elections for state senate and state assembly offices take place every two years, with the primary in June and the general election in November. State Assembly seats have two-year terms and, therefore, those seats are up for election every two years. State senate seats have four-year terms. Half of the state senate seats are up for election every two years. The specific rotation of elections for these seats is discussed in chapter 6. The dates of local primary and general elections vary by locality. Finally, special elections can occur at various times of the year due to unexpected vacancies.

Direct Democracy

There are three types of mechanisms by which voters can have the final say on a matter of policy: initiatives, referenda, and recall attempts. Initiatives are employed in twenty-four states, and there is no primary for competing initiatives. Referenda are employed in all states, and recall elections are available to residents in eighteen states.[9]

The Initiative

Initiatives got their name because they are policy proposals that are initiated by individuals or groups, not by the state legislature. There are two types of initiatives: statute and constitutional. Voters decide whether a statute initiative may become part of the California Code and whether a constitution initiative may become part of the California Constitution. To place a statute initiative on the ballot, supporters must collect petition signatures equivalent to or greater than 5 percent of the total votes cast in the most recent gubernatorial election. Using the 2014 gubernatorial election as the baseline, the 5 percent threshold is 375,699 signatures. The signature requirement for a constitution initiative is 8 percent. Once again using the 2014 figures, the 8 percent threshold is 601,118. If either initiative is placed on the ballot, it needs a majority vote to be approved.

The Referendum

On a referendum proposal, voters are asked to judge an action previously taken by the state legislature. There are three main types of referenda: statute, constitutional, and mandatory. A statute referendum is proposed when an individual or group wishes to remove an element from the California Code that was enacted by the legislature. The qualifying procedure is identical to that for a statute initiative, and if a majority of voters approves the referendum, the statute is removed from the California Code.

The remaining two types of referenda are placed on the ballot by the legislature. A constitutional referendum is placed on the ballot by a two-thirds vote of each chamber—twenty-seven in the senate, fifty-four in the assembly—with each chamber voting separately. If a majority of voters approves the measure, it becomes part of the California Constitution. A mandatory referendum is also placed on the ballot after a two-thirds vote from each chamber. Mandatory referenda involve the approval of government bonds, which are used to fund large construction projects or other significant capital outlays. These referenda are called "mandatory" because the legislature and the governor cannot issue bonds that are backed by taxpayer dollars unless the measure is approved by the voters. However, urgency measures (which are discussed in chapter 6, on the legislature) are exempt from the referendum process.

The Recall

State and local officers can be removed before the expiration of their term by means of a recall petition and election. In order for a recall election to take place, supporters must obtain a minimum number of signatures, and the amount required to force an election varies with the office. For directly elected executives, except for the four district representatives on the state Board of Equalization, the number of signatures must be at least 12 percent of the total votes cast in the most recent election for that office, with the further stipulation that the signatures must be collected from at least five counties. For state legislators, members of the Board of Equalization, and appellate court judges, the signatures must equal at least 20 percent of the total votes cast in the last election for that office. For local officials, the number of signatures required varies with the size of the locality:

30 percent if the voter registration is less than one thousand,

25 percent if the registration is less than ten thousand but at least one thousand,

20 percent if the registration is less than fifty thousand but at least ten thousand,

15 percent if the registration is less than one hundred thousand but at least fifty thousand,

10 percent if the registration is one hundred thousand or above.[10]

If enough signatures are collected, two separate questions are placed on the ballot. The first is whether the officer should be recalled. The second asks for a replacement officeholder should a majority of those voting choose to recall the sitting officeholder. If a majority decides to recall the officer, the person receiving the most votes on the second question takes office. Recall elections are rare and are more common for local officials than for state officials. However, such actions need not be frequent to be memorable, and their impact can be profound and last for decades. The memory of just one such election removing a colleague can lead an officeholder to abandon any notions of drifting too far from the sentiments of the constituents. The 2003 recall of Governor Gray Davis and the election of his replacement, Arnold Schwarzenegger, will reverberate through the American polity for decades.

Memorable Initiatives

As of 2012, ballot propositions will appear only on a general election ballot—in both presidential and gubernatorial years (2014, 2016, 2018, etc.).
Californians face a barrage of proposals in the form of initiatives and referenda, and a typical general election ballot contains several proposals.[11] Very
often, the initiative or referendum process is used by governors, legislators,
and interest groups to obtain desired policy goals after failing to enact them
in the normal legislative process. In fact, a huge commercial enterprise has
developed around direct democracy in California. Petition gathering, polling,
legal counseling, and campaign consulting amount to a major industry in the
Golden State. The situation is so complex that sometimes a group or official
opposed to a policy idea successfully places an initiative on the ballot, hoping
for it to be defeated!

Even though the system is complex, direct democracy remains popular
with the people of California.[12] Some of the more memorable initiatives
that have passed concerned property tax relief (Proposition 13, 1978), term
limits (Proposition 140, 1990), illegal immigration (Proposition 187, 1994),
the scaling back of affirmative action (Proposition 209, 1996), the scaling
back of bilingual education (Proposition 227, 1998), approving casino gambling (Proposition 5, 1998), state funding of stem cell research (Proposition
71, 2004), "Jessica's Law," which places increased residency restrictions
on convicted sex offenders (Proposition 83, 2006), prohibition on same-
sex marriage (Proposition 8, 2008), citizen redistricting commission for
state legislative seats (Proposition 11, 2008), "top two" primary elections
(Proposition 14, 2010), simple majority vote in legislature for state budgets
(Proposition 25, 2010), and a weakening of California's Three Strikes Law
(Proposition 36, 2012). Unless the initiative is drafted otherwise, most are
required to go into effect immediately on passage—unless, of course, the
proposal is struck down in the courts.

The Role of the Courts

Even if the voters approve an initiative, it may still be invalidated in a federal or state court. Most of the time, it is the federal courts that act to strike
down California initiatives. One reason for this could be the fact that state
judges must stand for voter approval, while federal judges have lifetime appointments and thus have less to lose by making unpopular decisions.

A prominent example of judicial interference occurred with Proposition
187, which was approved by voters in 1994. Proposition 187, which was
backed strongly by Governor Pete Wilson (1991–1999), sought to eliminate
the state's financial responsibility for providing health care and education

to illegal immigrants. This measure was invalidated with an immediate injunction in federal court and was never implemented. In the minds of many, the court system acts as an additional check on the direct democracy system, much like the checks and balances in the legislative process between the senate, assembly, and governor. However, there is some doubt as to whether this "judicial check" is in line with what the Founders had intended for American democracy. The checks and balances of the federal system were designed to promote rational deliberation so that the reasoned judgment of the public would emerge.[13]

Vital Election Statistics

Campaign Finance

California elections can be expensive. The two major candidates in the 2014 gubernatorial election were Neel Kashkari, the Republican nominee, and incumbent Jerry Brown, the Democratic nominee. Neel Kashkari, a successful businessman and former Assistant Secretary of the Treasury, spent approximately $7 million. The winner, Jerry Brown, spent approximately $5 million. Therefore, total spending in the 2014 gubernatorial elections was about $12 million.[14] But this is small compared to the 2010 election when Meg Whitman, the wealthy former head of EBay, spent more than $170 million dollars in defeat, most of which was her own money, while Jerry Brown, the eventual winner, spent $36 million. In 1976, when Jerry Brown defeated Evelle Younger to win the gubernatorial election, total spending for both candidates was $5,709,806.[15] This is a dramatic increase, even when inflation is considered.[16] What is to be done about this? Some would argue that states must impose a spending cap and that these expensive races limit the ability of the non-elite to participate in the system. According to this belief, campaign money is property and can be regulated by the government.

There is, however, another side of this argument. Instead of being viewed as property, campaign money can be viewed as a form of speech; as such, it is protected by both the California and U.S. constitutions. If limits are placed on how much money a candidate can spend in an election, then those limits can, in effect, harm the ability of a candidate to present a message to voters and thus limit the candidate's right to free speech.[17] Furthermore, spending limits would favor incumbents, who already have an advantage in name recognition and media exposure, and place a burden on challengers.[18] To overcome the power of incumbents, challengers must often spend more than the incumbent. However, the successful implementation of term limits in California has made elections more accessible to challengers.[19]

Voter Turnout

Voter turnout can be measured in two ways: One method is to calculate the number of voters as a percentage of the voting-age population. Out of all the people who were eligible to vote, which voters actually showed up at the polls? Another method is to calculate the number of voters as a percentage of those registered. Historically, there is a significant difference between the two figures. Voter turnout as a percentage of registered voters has consistently been above the 70 percent mark, while turnout as a percentage of the population has been at or below 50 percent since 1970. Why the difference? It takes time to register, and registration must take place at least fifteen days before the election. One cannot simply show up at the polls the day of the election and vote. Finally, turnout is much greater in state elections that coincide with a presidential election because people are more likely to vote during larger elections.

Voter turnout in the 2014 California general elections was just under 31 percent of eligible voters, a record low for a general election in the Golden State.[20] Perhaps people are more distracted by the many forms of entertainment available to them or are cynical about government.[21] Perhaps the dominance of Democrats in California is so complete that general elections for statewide office are forgone conclusions and, accordingly, generate little voter interest. It remains to be seen if the record low turnout in 2014 was an aberration or a disturbing downward plunge from an already declining trend of voter participation. Declining turnout has led to a variety of efforts to reverse this trend. However, one would assume that people would do more than "turn out" for an election; one might hope that they would also make a well-informed decision, based on their own preferences and understanding of issues.

Issue Highlight for Chapter 5: Recall of Gray Davis

Governor Gray Davis, a Democrat, was unpopular heading into his 2002 reelection campaign. The public was unhappy with his handling of the electricity blackouts and the state budget. However, his Republican challenger, Bill Simon, made campaign errors no experienced politician would make. Davis beat Simon by a 47–42 percent vote. Nonetheless, the low voter turnout and relative closeness of the race were signs of weakness for Davis. Then, after the election, Davis allowed that the state budget deficit was much higher than he had maintained—$38 billion. Gray Davis was widely perceived as inept and having gained reelection through dishonesty about the size of the state deficit.

The movement against Davis reached critical mass in May 2003. Republican Congressman Darrell Issa—a former entrepreneur and multimillion-aire—poured $2 million of his personal funds into a recall petition drive that antitax activist Ted Costa began in February. Initially opposed or downplayed by the Republican establishment, the recall drive gained momentum over the summer, with over a million signatures, and was officially certified on July 23.

October 7 was set as the day for this special election, in which the ballot asked voters to decide two questions: whether Davis should be retained as governor and who should replace him in the event of his recall. The state constitution provided that Davis had to win a majority of votes to retain his seat. If he failed, the top vote-getter on the second half of the question would become the new governor.

Hollywood action star Arnold Schwarzenegger, a Republican, surprised even his own staff and announced on the *Tonight Show* with Jay Leno that he would enter the race. As the relatively brief campaign wore on, Schwarzenegger's most serious challengers were Lieutenant Governor Cruz Bustamante, the lone Democrat among the major candidates, and State Senator Tom McClintock, a conservative Republican who had barely lost the 2002 election for controller. Davis could not use the abortion or gay rights issues against his main Republican opponent as he had in previous elections—Schwarzenegger is fairly liberal on hot-button social issues. The focus of the election remained on state finances. On election day, the recall won 55–45 percent. On the second part of the ballot, Schwarzenegger took 49 percent of the vote, Bustamante 32 percent, and fellow Republican McClintock 13 percent.[22] Arnold Schwarzenegger would become governor of the nation's most populous state.

Gray Davis's loss in the recall election was a tremendous blow to a proud and once-mighty politician. Davis had served as special assistant to Los Angeles mayor Tom Bradley, gubernatorial chief of staff during Jerry Brown's first stint as governor, assembly member, controller, lieutenant governor, and governor. In addition, Davis was on Al Gore's short list of vice presidential picks in the 2000 presidential race and on the early watch list of potential 2004 presidential candidates. The fall of Gray Davis is one of the most stunning events in American political history.

Conclusion

Elections are the vital link between citizens and government. State and local elections afford a citizen the chance to decide matters that are close to home. In a sense, all elections are state elections because elections for the presidency,

Congress, governorship, state legislature, state judiciary, and local offices are conducted by the states. The chief elections officer in California is the secretary of state, and elections occur in the state of California several times every year. There are two main types of elections for offices in California: primary elections and general elections. The winner of a primary election runs against another finalist in a general election. The winner of a general election attains office. Initiatives, referenda, and recall attempts can be placed on an election ballot for voter approval.

6

The Legislature

When . . . public power is in the hands of the people, the sovereign seeks everywhere for what is better because it feels bad itself. The spirit of improvement then spreads to a thousand diverse objects; it descends to infinite details, and above all it is applied to the kinds of improvement that can only be obtained by paying.[1]

PROGRESSIVISM'S INFLUENCE IS especially pronounced in the character of California's legislature, one of America's leading examples of a "professional legislature."[2] A legislature is considered "professional" if its members have high salaries, are supported by a large staff, and convene in lengthy regular sessions.[3] The California legislature is among the most professional in the nation, along with Florida, Illinois, Massachusetts, Michigan, New York, Ohio, Pennsylvania, and Wisconsin. California's senate and assembly are regularly in session, throughout the year. They have large staffs.[4] California's senate and assembly members earn annual compensation of approximately $100,000. On the other hand, the legislators in Texas—a large complex state like California—serve only 140 days, every other year, and receive an annual salary of about $7,000 plus expenses.[5]

Legislation as Practical Wisdom

The Nature of Political Decisions

The term *legislature* is derived from the Latin *legis lator*, which means a "proposer of law." Laws are decisions about the public good and how best to pursue it.[6] Laws are enforced by the government's coercive authority, the legitimate power to take life. For example, nothing could be more mundane than a driver's license; almost every eligible Californian has this small piece of plastic that allows us the privilege of driving to the movies, the grocery store, or school. These are all ordinary things, but being caught operating an automobile without one would prove to be anything but ordinary. At the very least, one would receive a ticket, which would be noted on one's driving record. With the ticket, the government would levy a substantial fine, and if the fine were not paid, the person fined would be subject to arrest and imprisonment. Inmates are incarcerated under the watch of armed guards—persons authorized to possess lethal force, which is the power to take life. Therefore, even an ordinary driver's license is a reminder of the ultimate power of the government.

Legislation in a Republic

Besides its final and most extreme character, legislation in a republic has another dimension: the ability of constituents to judge their representatives' actions. The final determination of whether elected officials have deliberated in society's best interest rests with the voters.[7] For voters to make informed judgments on the merits of their elected officers, they must be able to comprehend adequately the legislation on which the representative decided. A voter must be able to identify specific issues before the legislature and assess their representative's position.[8] This idea is the core of the American polity.[9]

However, in California the deliberative process is short-circuited to some extent. California's initiative process takes many of the more controversial—not to mention interesting—issues out of the hands of legislators and places them directly before the voters. On the one hand, this initiative process can be seen as a detriment to legislators, for direct democracy diminishes the stature of the legislature as a representative body. On the other hand, direct democracy protects legislators' career interests because they can more easily avoid taking a stand on a controversial matter that might come back to haunt them at the next election.

The Bicameral System

The California legislature is bicameral, like the U.S. Congress and forty-nine of the fifty state legislatures.[10] This means that the legislature is divided into two decision-making bodies: a forty-member senate and an eighty-member assembly. Bicameralism serves a vital function in a republic, and Tocqueville described it as a "necessity of the first order."[11] Modern political science scholarship confirms the ancient understanding that bicameralism reduces the potential instability of republican governments.[12] People have little respect for an institution that makes frantic and illogical decisions, which are more possible under unicameral governments.[13] Under bicameralism, it is more difficult for a single group to control the entire process, which ensures a more stable policy system that is more likely to produce a reverence for the rule of law, a necessary condition for political life.[14]

Districting

The method of representation in California's assembly has always been on the basis of population, with eighty assembly districts of equal population. From 1926 until 1966, representation in the senate was based on geography. The state was divided into forty districts that contained whole counties or groups of counties, regardless of population. Some state senators had districts with large populations, while others had small ones. In *Baker v. Carr* (1962), *Reynolds v. Sims* (1964), and *Wesberry v. Sanders* (1964), the U.S. Supreme Court declared that such plans of representation violated the Fourteenth Amendment's requirement for "equal protection under the laws." In the opinion of the court, the individual votes of those living in a senate district of fifteen thousand people were more powerful than those living in a senate district of three million.

Through these decisions, the Supreme Court established the principle of "one man, one vote."[15] States must define the representation in both chambers of their legislatures on the basis of population, with each district being as equal as possible.[16] As a result, California's senate is divided into forty districts, each containing approximately 900,000, and its assembly is divided into eighty districts, each containing about 450,000 people.[17] Every ten years, California must redraw its legislative districts to ensure that they are, for the most part, equally populated.

Conflicts over Redistricting

As one might imagine, redistricting has been a highly controversial procedure. The manner in which a district is drawn could determine whether a Republican or a Democrat is elected from that district. The redrawing of districts for political advantage is known as *gerrymandering*, which in California has been an ongoing source of controversy. The first installment of this drama occurred after the 1970 census, when the Democrat-controlled legislature produced a redistricting plan that was vetoed by Republican governor Ronald Reagan.[18] The impasse was eventually resolved by a court-ordered redistricting plan.

The second installment of the drama occurred after the 1980 census, when the Democrat-controlled legislature presented Democrat governor Jerry Brown with a plan that he eventually signed. However, the Republicans fought back with a series of successful ballot initiatives that invalidated the plan. As was the case in the 1970s, the courts intervened to impose a new districting plan.

The third installment of the drama mirrored the first: In the 1990s, a Democrat-controlled legislature presented Republican governor Pete Wilson with a plan that he vetoed. After a series of ballot initiatives and counter-proposals by the legislature, the courts, once again, imposed a districting plan. The redistricting plan after the 2000 census was less contentious. This was not because Democrats and Republicans had set aside their differences. Instead, the ease with which the plan was implemented had more to do with unified Democratic control over the legislature and governor's mansion and the GOP's failure to challenge the plan in court.

With the passage of Proposition 11 in 2008, redistricting in California enters another phase. Legislators no longer redraw their own lines after each census. Instead, Proposition 11 created a fourteen-member Citizen Redistricting Commission that will draw lines. The commission consists of private citizens. Five of them must be registered Democrats, five must be Republicans, and four members must be from another party or have no partisan affiliation. The selection process is coordinated by the State Auditor, with input from leaders in both political parties.[19]

Terms

California senators are elected to four-year terms and California assembly members are elected to two-year terms. As a result of a ballot initiative (Proposition 25, 2012), members of the state legislature are limited to a total of twelve years in office. The twelve years can be spent in one chamber or both. For example, if a legislator served four two-year terms in the assembly—for a total of eight years in the assembly—and then was elected to the senate, he or she would only be allowed to serve one four-year term in the senate.[20] As in other states, debate continues over the wisdom of term limits. California, along with Oklahoma, has the most restrictive legislative term limits in the nation.[21] By increasing the turnover of legislative members, does one increase the power of the governor, other members of the executive branch, career government staff, and interest groups? Is California's government better served? The answers remain to be seen, as term limits are still relatively new.

Partisan Division and Organization

The assembly and the senate each convene on the first Monday in December in even-numbered years. The two-year period between each convocation is known as a "legislative session." At the beginning of each two-year "session," the members of each chamber organize themselves into a *majority caucus*, which contains those members from the chamber's majority party, and a *minority caucus*, which contains those members from the chamber's minority party.[22]

The Speaker of the Assembly

The presiding officers of the assembly are the speaker of the assembly, the majority leader, and the minority leader. The majority and minority leaders are elected by their own party caucuses, and the entire chamber elects the speaker. Like the speaker of the U.S. House, the speaker of the assembly will almost always be a member of the majority party: after a series of straw polls, the majority caucus unites behind one candidate. A historic exception to this rule occurred after the 1994 elections. The Republicans had won a rare and narrow victory over the Democrats and took control of the assembly. However, Assemblyman Paul Horcher, a Republican, defected to the Democratic side, leaving longtime GOP nemesis Willie Brown, a Democrat, as the speaker. Horcher was eventually recalled, and the Republicans regained control of the chamber. However, Doris Allen, another Republican defector, switched sides and tilted effective control of the chamber to the Democrats until she, too, was recalled by her constituents.

The speaker has effective control over who will sit on committees, the assignment of particular bills to committees, who will be recognized on the floor of the chamber, and the amount of financial support members of the majority caucus will receive in their next reelection bid.

President Pro Tempore of the Senate

The titular head of the senate is the lieutenant governor, which mirrors the dual role of the vice president of the United States as president of the senate. Like the vice president, the lieutenant governor rarely becomes involved in legislative affairs. The lieutenant governor's only major legislative responsibility is to cast a deciding vote in the case of a tie.

The effective head of the senate is the president pro tempore—most often referred to as the president pro tem. The most influential member of the majority caucus is usually elected president pro tem. He or she chairs the senate

Rules Committee, which acts as the main governing body of the chamber and supervises such duties as assigning committee seats and monitoring the flow of bills. While not approaching the same relative level of power as the speaker, the president pro tem has become a more pivotal figure in the legislative process in recent years. This is a result of the legacy of David Roberti, the president pro tem of the Democrat-controlled senate of the 1980s. Senator Roberti's skill and energy set a precedent for subsequent presidents pro tem.

Legislative Process

The legislative process, by which bills can become laws, has five stages: introducing a bill, committee consideration, floor consideration, consideration in the other chamber, and consideration by the governor.[23] Only sitting legislators can introduce legislation in the assembly or senate. The governor, lieutenant governor, other government officials not in the legislature, and private citizens cannot introduce legislation into either the assembly or the senate. However, it is common for them to work closely with legislators in the drafting of legislation.

Introduction of a Bill

A legislator who thinks a policy proposal would make a good law drafts the idea into a formal document known as a *bill*. Generally speaking, a legislator will propose the broad outline of such a bill and leave it to staff members to fill in the details. Once the bill is drafted, it is then officially introduced into the chamber. The clerk of the chamber assigns it a number according to the order in which it was introduced. If the bill was introduced into the senate, then "SB"—senate bill—would appear before the number, and "AB" appears before the number on assembly bills. It is important to remember that a bill must pass in the same two-year session in which it was introduced. If a session expires before the bill is enacted into law, the bill must start over again when the next legislature convenes. For example, the legislature that convened in December 2012 will last until December 2014. If a bill is introduced in August 2013, it must become a law by December 2014, or it will need to be reintroduced in the next session.

Committee Consideration

The next step after introduction is committee consideration. The Rules Committee in each chamber assigns a bill to a committee according to the bill's subject matter. For example, an assembly farm bill would likely be assigned to that chamber's Agriculture Committee. A senate farm bill would go to the senate's Agriculture Committee.[24] It is the job of a committee to study the bill and decide whether it should be considered by the full chamber.

Committees are important institutions in each chamber (see table 6.1). They hold hearings, conduct studies, and assess the likelihood that a bill will have a reasonable chance of passage on a floor vote. Member and committee staffs analyze the legislation and lobbyists make their views known. In addition, a nonpartisan legislative analyst, who is appointed by the Joint

TABLE 6.1
Standing Committees, California Legislature

Assembly Committees	Senate Committees
Accountability and Administrative Review	Agriculture
Aging and Long-Term Care	Appropriations
Agriculture	Banking, Finance, and Insurance
Appropriations	Budget and Fiscal Review
Arts, Entertainment, Sports, Tourism, Internet Media	Business, Professions, Economic Development
Banking and Finance	Education
Budget	Elections, Constitutional Amendments
Business and Professions	Energy, Utilities and Communications
Education	Environmental Quality
Elections and Redistricting	Governance and Finance
Environmental Safety and Toxic Materials	Governmental Organization
Governmental Organization	Health
Health	Human Services
Higher Education	Insurance
Housing and Community Development	Judiciary
Human Services	Labor and Industrial Relations
Insurance	Legislative Ethics
Jobs, Economic Development, Economy	Local Government
Judiciary	Natural Resources and Water
Labor and Employment	Public Employment and Retirement
Local Government	Public Safety
Natural Resources	Rules
Privacy and Consumer Protection	Transportation and Housing
Public Employees, Retirement, Social Security	Veterans Affairs
Public Safety	
Revenue and Taxation	
Rules	
Transportation	
Utilities and Commerce	
Veterans Affairs	
Water, Parks, and Wildlife	

Sources: California Assembly Committees, http://assembly.ca.gov/committees (accessed February 1, 2015); California Senate Committees, http://senate.ca.gov/committees (accessed February 1, 2015).

Legislative Budget Committee, provides members with budgetary, fiscal, and policy information. Committees act as filters through which hundreds of bills must pass. Because it is physically impossible for the legislature to vote on every bill introduced in each chamber, most bills are not approved by committees for floor consideration.[25]

Floor Vote and Consideration in the Other Chamber

If a bill survives the committee process, it is brought to the floor for full consideration by the chamber. A majority vote of the entire membership is required for the bill to survive—twenty-one in the senate and forty-one in the assembly.[26] If the bill receives a majority vote, it is sent to the other chamber, where it is reintroduced. If the bill is approved by a majority vote in the other chamber without amending the version sent to it by the original chamber, it is enrolled as an "act of the legislature" and sent to the governor. However, if the other chamber made changes to the bill, the original chamber must agree to these changes or a conference committee will need to be convened. In a conference committee, three members from each chamber meet to produce a single, identical bill that could be sent to each chamber. If no compromise can be reached, the bill dies. If a compromise is reached and each chamber approves an identical bill, it is sent to the governor.

Consideration by the Governor

When receiving a bill, the governor has three options: (1) sign the act, which would make it law; (2) do nothing and allow the act to become law without a signature; (3) veto the act, which means that the act could only become law if the legislature, voting separately in each chamber, supported it with a two-thirds vote.[27]

If an act becomes a law, it will go into effect on the following January 1, as long as ninety days have expired since it was approved. Exceptions to this rule are known as *urgency measures*, which, if approved by the governor, go into effect immediately. However, a two-thirds vote is required of each chamber in order to send an urgency measure to the governor. Other legislation requiring two-thirds approval are tax increases, constitutional amendments, and senate impeachment trials.

Case Study for Chapter 6: "Gut and Amend"

In the earlier section on legislative committees, we described the normal legislative process for bills. The purpose of a committee is to study a bill, seek public input, and assess whether the bill has a decent chance to receive majority support in a floor vote. However, legislators have been known to short-circuit this process in their haste to pass bills before the end of a session.

In a last-minute effort to pass a bill before the legislature adjourns, lawmakers sometimes use a tactic called "gut and amend." A moribund bill is stripped of its title and language. All that remains is the bill number. The title and language are then replaced with something different. For example, in 2014 Assemblyman Mike Gatto (D–Glendale) had a water reservoir bill stripped of its title and language. In its place, Gatto inserted language that would modify the rules for gun buyback programs. In another example, Governor Pete Wilson, a Republican, led an effort to enact a $931 million tax cut in 1997 through the gut and amend process. Both Republicans and Democrats have used the "gut and amend" procedure. However, there is cause for concern about how this technique has been used in recent years.[28]

It was once the case that a six-person committee of members from both chambers had to approve the "gutting and amending" of a bill. In addition, the changes had to be related to the original language of the bill. That is no longer true. Gutted bills get hasty hearings with little chance for the public to participate. For example, as the session drew to a close in late August 2006, no less than seven senate committees met during a short forty-minute span. In response to questions about his use of the "gut and amend" procedure to replace a $1 increase in the minimum wage with provisions granting driver's licenses to illegal immigrants, Assemblyman Lloyd Levine (D–Van Nuys) said that "it's not about shenanigans. It's about trying to get public policy accomplished and sometimes we do that the best way that we can and in this case, we had to find a different vehicle."[29]

This process has received scathing criticism from political pundits on both sides of the political spectrum. One editorialist claimed that "political insiders in Sacramento would just as soon keep quiet about the disturbingly common practice of gutting and amending a bill in order to slip it through at the very end of a legislative session."[30] Speaking of "gut and amend," the editorialist also wrote that "California students won't find it in their civics textbooks."

Conclusion

The California legislature is one of the most professional state legislatures in the United States. Like the U.S. Congress and forty-nine of the fifty state legislatures, it is bicameral. It is divided into a forty-member senate and an eighty-member assembly. Redistricting plans are proposed every ten years following the census and are often surrounded by partisan controversy. California Senate members are elected to four-year terms. California Assembly members are elected to two-year terms. The presiding assembly officer is the speaker, and the effective presiding senate officer is the president pro tem.

The legislative process has five stages: introduction of a bill, committee consideration, floor consideration, consideration in the other chamber, and consideration by the governor. The governor, lieutenant governor, other government officials not in the legislature, and private citizens cannot introduce legislation into either the assembly or the senate. The Rules Committee assigns a bill to a committee according to the bill's subject matter. If a bill survives the committee process, it is brought to the floor for full consideration by the chamber. If an identical bill is not approved by the other chamber, the bill dies. If the other chamber approves the bill, the governor can sign it, allow it to become law without a signature, or veto it.

7

The Executive

The executive power of the state has the governor for representative. It is not by chance that I have picked this word, representative. The governor of the state in fact represents the executive power; but he exercises only some of its rights.[1]

THE EXECUTIVE BRANCH OF the State of California is entrusted with the implementation of laws that have been passed by California or that have been mandated by the federal government. The term *executive* is derived from the Latin word *exsequor*, which means "to carry out." California's executive branch is more fragmented than is the executive branch of the federal government. Whereas the president of the United States is the sole elected head of the federal executive branch, the leadership of California's executive branch is divided among a number of elected officials. This shared responsibility is known as a **plural executive**. Furthermore, the governor's powers over the executive branch are limited by California's civil service system, which has been in place since 1913.[2] A strong civil service system is a key element of the form of administration called a **bureaucracy**. California's executive branch is one of the most bureaucratic in the nation and its level of bureaucratization is a result of the rise of Progressivism since the late nineteenth century.

California's Governor

According to article 5, section 1 of the state constitution, "The supreme executive power of this state is vested in the governor. The governor shall see that the law is faithfully executed." The power of the governor, however, to execute these laws is diffused by the plural executive system. The governor does not have a cabinet in the same sense that the president of the United States does. The federal cabinet consists of the heads of the top fifteen executive departments; assuming that the Senate approves the cabinet appointees (and such nominations are almost always approved), the president appoints members of the cabinet and has the power to remove them at any time. Therefore, the president has a great deal of control over the policies of the federal executive branch.

The governor of California, on the other hand, cannot remove the heads of the state's most important departments: attorney general, secretary of state, treasurer, controller, superintendent of public instruction, and insurance commissioner. These officials are elected by the voters. However, the governor can appoint people to these directly elected offices, as well as to California's two U.S. Senate seats, when an unexpected vacancy occurs.

Terms and Elections

According to article 5, section 2 of the state constitution, the governor is limited to two four-year terms. Governor Jerry Brown, however, is an exception to the two-term limit. He served two four-year terms as governor, from 1975 to 1983. Since term limits were enacted after he left office (Proposition 140 in 1990), he is allowed to seek two more additional terms, the first of which he was elected to in 2010.[3] (Table 7.1 lists California governors from 1849 to the present.) Gubernatorial elections are held in even-numbered, nonpresidential election years, such as 2010, 2014, and 2018. Once in office, a governor can nominate the heads of agencies and departments that do not have directly elected officials. Most of these nominations, however, require legislative approval. The governor also appoints members of the state court of appeals and supreme court, on confirmation by a judicial commission. The governor also appoints judges when vacancies appear in a county's superior court.

Veto

As described in chapter 6, the governor may exercise a veto over an act of the legislature. The governor may sign a bill into law, veto it and send it back to the legislature, or allow it to become law without a signature. All gubernatorial vetoes are subject to legislative override. With a two-thirds vote by each legislature chamber, a bill can become law without a governor's signa-

TABLE 7.1
California Governors

Name	Party	In Office
Peter H. Burnett	Indep. Democrat	1849–1851
John McDougal	Indep. Democrat	1851–1852
John Bigler	Democrat	1852–1856
James Neeley Johnson	American	1856–1858
John B. Weller	Democrat	1858–1860
Milton S. Latham	Lecompton Democrat	1860[a]
John G. Downey	Lecompton Democrat	1860–1862
Leland Stanford	Republican	1862–1863
Frederick F. Low	Union	1863–1867
Henry H. Haight	Democrat	1867–1871
Newton Booth	Republican	1871–1875
Romulado Pacheco	Republican	1875
William Irwin	Democrat	1875–1880
George C. Perkins	Republican	1880–1883
George Stoneman	Democrat	1883–1887
Washington Bartlett	Democrat	1887
Robert W. Waterman	Republican	1887–1891
Henry H. Markham	Republican	1891–1895
James H. Budd	Democrat	1895–1899
Henry T. Gage	Republican	1899–1903
George Pardee	Republican	1903–1907
James N. Gillett	Republican	1907–1911
Hiram W. Johnson	Republican	1911–1915
Hiram W. Johnson	Progressive	1915–1917
William D. Stephens	Republican	1917–1923
Friend W. Richardson	Republican	1923–1927
Clement C. Young	Republican	1927–1931
James Rolph Jr.	Republican	1931–1934
Frank F. Merriam	Republican	1934–1939
Culbert L. Olson	Democrat	1939–1943
Earl Warren	Republican	1943–1953
Goodwin J. Knight	Republican	1953–1959
Edmund G. Brown Sr.	Democrat	1959–1967
Ronald W. Reagan	Republican	1967–1975
Edmund G. Brown Jr.	Democrat	1975–1983
George Deukmejian	Republican	1983–1991
Pete Wilson	Republican	1991–1999
Gray Davis	Democrat	1999–2003[b]
Arnold Schwarzenegger	Republican	2003–2011[c]
Edmund G. Brown Jr.	Democrat	2011–[d]

[a]A Lecompton Democrat supported a pro-slavery Kansas Constitution. The issue split the Democratic Party.

[b]Gray Davis was recalled from office.

[c]Arnold Schwarzenegger was the top candidate on the replacement ballot in the recall election. Schwarzenegger won reelection in 2006 and was not eligible to run again in 2010.

[d]Term limits for governors were enacted in 1990 as a result of the passage of Proposition 140. Edmund G. Brown Jr. served two four-year terms from 1975 to 1983. He is allowed to serve two more four-year terms because term limits went into effect after he had left office.

Source: List of California Governors, http://www.sandiegohistory.org/books/pourade/data/governors4.htm (accessed January 9, 2011).

ture. However, such overrides are rare, and vetoes are relatively uncommon. Historically, about 10 percent of all bills presented to the governor receive a veto. This is not to say that the veto is rarely used because it is ineffective.[4] The threat of a veto can affect legislation as it moves through the senate and assembly. Wise legislators, therefore, would be remiss if they did not anticipate the policy preferences of governors.

Budget

California has what is known as an **executive budget**. State agencies and departments cannot submit budget requests directly to the legislature but must submit their proposals to the governor. The governor then crafts a unified budget, which is presented to the legislature as a single document. This gives the governor a great deal of leverage over public policy. An even greater form of political leverage is gained by the **line item veto**, with which the governor may veto specific portions of the legislature's annual budget bill without casting a veto against the entire budget. The legislature may still try to override a veto over a particular line item, but since such overrides are rare, the governor can effectively eliminate items from the budget. Other significant powers of the governor include being the commander in chief of the California National Guard. The National Guard can be called out in an emergency to ensure public order.

In addition to the preceding *formal powers* of the governor, which are shared by governors of most other states, the governor of California has a very important *informal power* that is virtually unique to the Golden State. As the top elected official of the most populous state, California's governor is automatically vaulted to the upper echelon of national politics and is almost always a serious player in presidential elections. Governor Ronald Reagan (1967–1975) was considered a possible contender for the Republican nomination in 1968, nearly defeated incumbent President Gerald Ford for the Republican nomination in 1976, then went on to receive the nomination in 1980, and was successfully elected twice as the fortieth president of the United States. Governor Jerry Brown (1975–1983) was a serious contender for the Democratic nomination for president in 1976, winning several primaries.[5] For a few months in 1976, there was talk that both the Democratic and Republican nominees in that year's presidential election would have been current or former governors of California.[6] Governor Brown ran again in 1992 and was the last man standing out of the five challengers to the eventual nominee, Arkansas governor Bill Clinton.

Governors Pete Wilson and Gray Davis continued in this prominent role. Until withdrawing his candidacy just before the New Hampshire primary in 1996, Governor Pete Wilson (1991–1999) was a candidate for president.

Governor Gray Davis was a top contender for the vice presidential spot on the 2000 Democratic ticket, a spot that was eventually filled by Senator Joseph Lieberman of Connecticut.[7] Arnold Schwarzenegger did not play a similar role. Foreign-born citizens are prohibited from assuming the presidency and vice presidency.

Other Elected Executives

California has a plural executive system. These directly elected executives are chosen in the same manner as the governor and adhere to the same term limits and election schedule (see table 7.2). The lieutenant governor assumes the office of governor upon a vacancy in that office. In addition to the role as the second in command, the lieutenant governor is the president of the California Senate. The activity of the lieutenant governor in this respect is usually limited to the occasional tiebreaking vote. The lieutenant governor also serves on the University of California Board of Regents, the California State University Board of Trustees, and the State Lands Commission. Furthermore, the lieutenant governor chairs the California Commission for Economic Development.[8] The attorney general of California is the state's top legal officer and the chief legal counsel for all state agencies and departments. The attorney general represents the state in all lawsuits, as either a plaintiff or defendant, and is also the top official in charge of district attorneys and sheriffs.[9] The secretary of state is the chief elections officer in California and the official custodian of California's public records. With California's massive initiative, referendum, and recall system, this is a high-profile position within state government. The treasurer is the state's chief financial officer and has official possession of state tax revenues until they are earmarked by the budget. The treasurer is in charge of all state investments, including selling bonds, and has the official capacity to borrow money on behalf of the state.[10] The controller disburses state money and acts as the chief auditor for the state.[11] The controller is also on the Board of Equalization, along with four other members, directly elected from California's four equalization districts. The role of the Board of Equalization is to ensure that assessment levels for local property taxes are not set at radically different levels throughout the state. The insurance commissioner is charged with oversight of the insurance industry and must approve rate changes. The superintendent of public instruction is unique among California's elected executives because it is the only such office that is elected on a nonpartisan basis.[12] The superintendent is the head of the Department of Education and the chief executive officer of the Board of Education. Therefore, the superintendent is the top official in California's public school system.[13]

TABLE 7.2
California Elected Executives: 1945 to Present

Officeholder	Party	Years in Office
Lieutenant Governor		
Frederick F. Houser	Republican	1943–1947
Goodwin J. Knight	Republican	1947–1953
Harold J. Powers	Republican	1953–1959
Glenn M. Anderson	Democrat	1959–1967
Robert H. Finch	Republican	1967–1969
Ed Reinecke	Republican	1969–1974
John L. Harmer	Republican	1974–1975
Mervyn M. Dymally	Democrat	1975–1979
Mike Curb	Republican	1979–1983
Leo T. McCarthy	Democrat	1983–1995
Gray Davis	Democrat	1995–1999
Cruz Bustamante	Democrat	1999–2007
John Garamendi	Democrat	2007–2009
Abel Maldonado	Republican	2010–2011
Gavin Newsom	Democrat	2011–
Attorney General		
Robert W. Kenny	Democrat	1943–1947
Fred N. Howser	Republican	1947–1951
Edmund G. Brown Sr.	Democrat	1951–1959
Stanley Mosk	Democrat	1959–1964
Thomas C. Lynch	Democrat	1964–1971
Evelle J. Younger	Republican	1971–1979
George Deukmejian	Republican	1979–1983
John Van De Kamp	Democrat	1983–1991
Daniel E. Lungren	Republican	1991–1999
Bill Lockyer	Democrat	1999–2007
Edmund G. Brown Jr.	Democrat	2007–2011
Kamala Harris	Democrat	2011–
Secretary of State		
Frank M. Jordan	Republican	1943–1970
H.P. Sullivan	Republican	1970–1971
Edmund G. Brown Jr.	Democrat	1971–1975
March Fong Eu	Democrat	1975–1993
Tony Miller	Democrat	1993–1995
Bill Jones	Republican	1995–2003
Kevin Shelley	Democrat	2003–2005
Bruce McPherson	Republican	2005–2007
Debra Bowen	Democrat	2007–2015
Alex Padilla	Democrat	2015–
Treasurer		
Charles G. Johnson	Republican	1923–1956
Ronald A. Button	Republican	1956–1959

Officeholder	Party	Years in Office
Bert A. Betts	Democrat	1959–1967
Ivy Baker Priest	Republican	1967–1975
Jesse M. Unruh	Democrat	1975–1987
Vacant		1987–1988
Thomas Hayes	Republican	1988–1991
Kathleen Brown	Democrat	1991–1995
Matthew Fong	Republican	1995–1998
Phil Angelides	Democrat	1999–2007
Bill Lockyer	Democrat	2007–2015
John Chiang	Democrat	2015–

Controller

Harry B. Riley	Republican	1937–1946
Thomas Kuchel	Republican	1946–1953
Robert C. Kirkwood	Republican	1953–1959
Alan Cranston	Democrat	1959–1967
Houston H. Flournoy	Republican	1967–1975
Kenneth Cory	Democrat	1975–1987
Gray Davis	Democrat	1987–1995
Kathleen Connell	Democrat	1995–2003
Steve Westly	Democrat	2003–2007
John Chiang	Democrat	2007–2015
Betty T. Yee	Democrat	2015–

Supt. of Public Instruction

Roy Simpson	Nonpartisan	1945–1963
Maxwell Rafferty	Nonpartisan	1963–1971
Riles Johnson	Nonpartisan	1971–1983
Bill Honig	Nonpartisan	1983–1992
William Dawson	Nonpartisan	1992–1995
Delaine Eastin	Nonpartisan	1995–2003
Jack O'Connell	Nonpartisan	2003–2011
Tom Torlakson	Nonpartisan	2011–

Insurance Commissioner

John Garamendi	Democrat	1991–1995
Chuck Quackenbush	Republican	1995–2000
Harry Low	Democrat	2000–2003
John Garamendi	Democrat	2003–2007
Steve Poizner	Republican	2007–2011
Dave Jones	Democrat	2011–

Sources: Lieutenant Governor, http://www.ltg.ca.gov; Attorney General, http://oag.ca.gov; Secretary of State, http://www.ss.ca.gov/; Treasurer, http://www.treasurer.ca.gov; Superintendent of Public Instruction, http://www.cde.ca.gov/eo; Insurance Commissioner, http://www.insurance.ca.gov/ (accessed February 1, 2015).

Other Agencies and Departments

In addition to the departments headed by elected executives, there are a number of agencies and departments headed by appointed officials. Most of these officials are nominated by the governor and confirmed by the legislature. A select group of these agencies and departments are headed by members of the governor's cabinet. However, as stated earlier, the governor's cabinet does not have the same prestige as the president's cabinet does.

Bureaucracy

Whether an agency or department is headed by an elected executive or an appointed one, all are organized as **bureaucracies**. Bureaucracies are hierarchical organizations that are organized in three tiers: **operators, managers, and executives**.[14] Operators are the front-line people who "do the job"; in a police department, they would be the patrol officers and detectives; and in a university, they would be the professors. Managers are those who oversee the actions of operators, such as police lieutenants and university deans. Executives are those who are in charge of the overall level of strategic planning, such as police chiefs and university presidents. Bureaucracy is the dominant, almost universal, mode of societal organization in the modern world and certainly in California.

The social scientist Max Weber recognized the growth of this form of organization nearly a century ago.[15] Prior to that time, most societies were not organized bureaucratically. The predominant mode of organization was what Weber called "traditional." Traditional societies are based on personal loyalty, with very little separation between public and private life; in contrast, the intended goal of bureaucracy is to create an administration based on the separation of public and private affairs. The treasury of a nation governed according to a traditional society would be the personal property of a regime's rulers, and the treasury of a bureaucratic regime is strictly separate from the personal fortune of those in charge of the government. The treasury of California is not the personal fortune of the governor, who receives an annual salary from the state of around $170,000 per year. In fact, the governor is not even the highest-paid statewide public official. The president of the University of California System earns an annual salary of approximately $570,000.[16]

The transition from traditional to bureaucratic administration can be seen most clearly in the changes made in the method of hiring government employees. Prior to the Progressive movement (1880s–1920s), almost all of the government employees were hired on the basis of what was known as the *spoils system*. The political party that had been victorious in a gubernatorial election, for example, would have had the privilege of filling state government posts with their friends and allies. This system encouraged a high level of voter turnout. One can only imagine the turnout today if thousands of jobs depended on the result of a gubernatorial election. The weakness of this system, however, was its inherent corruption. To solve this dilemma, the leaders of the Progressive movement, of which Governor Hiram Johnson (1911–1917) was a major figure, proposed the creation of a civil service.[17]

The goal of the civil service was to replace a traditional state government with a bureaucratic one.[18] Hiring decisions in a civil service are supposed to be made on the basis of merit, not on political loyalty. The core principle of the civil service is that government officials should be neutral with respect to politics; they should simply do the job that needs to be done. The strength of this system is that it eliminates much of the corruption in government, but the weakness is that most of those who work in government are now beyond the reach of the voters. During the most recent change in governors, when Jerry Brown replaced Arnold Schwarzenegger, all but a fraction of the government employees remained in office.

Issue Highlight Chapter 7: Limits of Progressive Leadership

The world watched in amazement in October 2003 as California voters recalled Governor Gray Davis in the middle of his second term and replaced him with movie star Arnold Schwarzenegger. A recall election, along with the ability of citizens to vote directly on ballot initiatives, is one of the defining elements of a Progressive political system. Voters had grown tired of what they perceived as Davis's negligence in the face of the state's budgetary problems. Spending was out of control. In Schwarzenegger's first State of the State address, before a joint session of the California legislature, the former body builder promised aggressive solutions to California's problems: "Every governor proposes moving boxes around to reorganize government. I don't want to move the boxes around; I want to blow them up."[19]

Over the course of his first eighteen months in office, Schwarzenegger became frustrated with the lack of progress being made in crucial government reform proposals. The Democrats controlled both chambers of the state legislature by large margins and were opposed to his reform efforts. They resisted his plans to "blow up" the boxes of government. In his desire to implement radical change in government, the governor sought to go over the heads of the legislature through the use of another tool of Progressivism, the ballot initiative. Schwarzenegger took his case directly to the people. After all, the recall had placed him in office and he placed his trust in the power of his personality to convince voters to enact his reform program. The special election took place in November 2005 and the governor's proposals were defeated.

If the governor would have focused public attention on his battle with the legislature he might have been better served. Instead, he chose to take on the entire public employee establishment, which he correctly viewed as forming the core of the Democratic Party's support. However, the governor failed to convince voters that their desires for change, as reflected in the 2003 recall election, were connected to the issues on the ballot in the 2005 special election. Instead of being viewed as an agent for change, the governor appeared to many voters as attacking the benefits of teachers, nurses, firefighters, and police.[20] The powers of personality and direct democracy have limits.

The governor changed political direction in response to this defeat. In 2006, he moved to the political left. He signed a bill that required drastic cuts in greenhouse gases emitted in California, in response to what some have argued is a global warming crisis. In addition, he joined with leading figures in the Democratic Party and supported a series of bond issues that were placed on the November 2006 ballot. The bonds proposals called for increased funding for highways, ports, schools, and other public works. The bond proposals won by strong margins. In addition, Schwarzenegger won reelection in a landslide over a hapless Democrat challenger, Phil Angelides. While his reelection victory over Angelides was an important personal political triumph, Schwarzenegger's second term oversaw massive budget deficits, legislative gridlock, and low approval ratings, a situation similar to that which propelled voters to recall Gray Davis in the first place. The failure of his earlier reform efforts at balancing the state budget were compounded by the onset of the Great Recession in 2008. State unemployment rose to well over 10 percent. The governor forged a temporary alliance with leaders in the Democrat legislature, to the annoyance of many of his fellow Republicans. The governor and Democratic legislative leaders fashioned a series of ballot propositions and called for a special election in June 2009. The measures were a package of tax increases and spending reforms. The voters overwhelmingly rejected the measures. A period of stalemate ensued for the remainder of Schwarzenegger's second term. Democrats in the legislature refused to enact the cuts necessary to bring the state's budget under control and the Republicans refused to sanction tax increases. The budget measures that were passed were balanced on paper only, leaving sizable real deficits immediately after passage.

Due to the two-term limit on California governors, Schwarzenegger was ineligible to run for reelection in 2010. In the election, former Governor Jerry Brown, a Democrat, defeated Republican Meg Whitman. This is an amazing turn of events, in light of the excitement and energy of the 2003 recall election. The recall brought Schwarzenegger into office, the quintessential outsider and Hollywood megastar, to offer a fresh perspective on policymaking in the Golden State. By the end of the Schwarzenegger administration, voters were content to hand power back to a man who had first served as governor in 1975, well before Schwarzenegger was a major movie star. Given the ineffectiveness of the Schwarzenegger administration, according to the standard of its own lofty ambitions, is it any wonder that California voters were content to hand the reins over to Jerry Brown, the consummate career politician?

Conclusion

The executive branch of the State of California is entrusted with the implementation of laws that have been passed by the state or that have been mandated by the federal government. California's executive branch is more fragmented than the executive branch of the federal government because the leadership of California's executive is divided among a number of elected officers. Furthermore, gubernatorial powers over the executive branch are limited by the strong civil service system of California, which has been in place since 1913. However, the governor's power over the state budget is comparable, if not relatively stronger, than the president's power over the federal budget. The other elected executives are chosen in the same manner as the governor, adhering to the same term limits. In addition to the departments headed by elected executives, there are a number of agencies and departments headed by appointed officials. A select group of these agencies and departments are headed by members of the governor's cabinet.

8

The Courts

The American judge can only pronounce when there is litigation. He is never occupied except with a particular case; and in order to act he must always wait until he has been seised [presented with a legal dispute]. . . . The American judge therefore resembles perfectly the magistrates of other nations. . . . Nevertheless, he is vested with immense political power. . . . The cause of it is in this sole fact: Americans have recognized in judges the right to found their rulings on the *Constitution* rather than on the *laws.* In other words, they have permitted them not to apply laws that might appear to them unconstitutional.[1]

JUST AS TOCQUEVILLE SUGGESTS, we shall consider judges and constitutions together. The progressive features of the California Constitution and polity are sharpened by the state's courts. These courts are rather at odds with founding father Alexander Hamilton's view of the U.S. Supreme Court as "the least dangerous to the political rights of the Constitution." But all the branches of government have been transformed since the Progressive Era; it can no longer be said that courts generally "have neither force nor will but merely judgment."[2] Originally, Progressivism opposed the courts that struck down legislation in the name of property rights. But Progressives such as Supreme Court Justice Oliver Wendell Holmes (a hero to both liberals and conservatives today) were not Hamiltonian justices.[3] Despite the fact that most state court systems, California's included, provide for elected judges and justices, one appreciates nonetheless Hamilton's hope that judges possess qualities of firmness, fortitude, moderation, and integrity as they perform their "duty as faithful guardians of the Constitution."[4]

Hamilton's and Tocqueville's reflections on American judges apply partly to California's situation: our judges are more political, and the self-restraint and moderation of earlier times have been notably absent from all the branches in California's constitutional development. Tocqueville also thought the U.S. Constitution only changeable by the "will of the people following forms that have been established and in cases that have been foreseen."[5] Under Progressivism, the U.S. Constitution and state constitutions have ceased to be outgrowths of natural rights, and have become as mutable as ordinary legislation—as exemplified by California voters' powers of initiative and referendum. If a constitution can be altered by majority popular vote, then why object to courts that can further alter the constitution and all laws passed under it? And, to extend this logic further, why not elect judges, subject them to recall, and force them to campaign? Thus, California has put a new twist on Tocqueville's famous remark that "[t]here is almost no **political question** in the United States that is not resolved sooner or later into a judicial question."[6]

Types of Courts

Supreme Court

The California Supreme Court has long been eulogized for its contributions to the development of contemporary law—for example, about product liability laws that enable individuals to sue on account of obvious misuse of an otherwise safe product, such as a cup of hot coffee purchased at a fast-food restaurant. This **supreme court** has been praised and damned for its decisions. The fault lines have not necessarily followed traditional left versus right distinctions. For example, the late associate justice Stanley Mosk has been praised by liberals for his role in developing the notion of **"independent state grounds"** and for defending an activist court in the area of criminal law, but he has also won praise from conservatives for his uncompromising assault on racial preferences in *Bakke v. Regents of the University of California*, a position that was substantially toned down by the U.S. Supreme Court. The controversial decisions of the court have included drastic narrowing of the death penalty (now reversed), regulating higher standards of guilt in criminal prosecutions, defending its own use of independent state grounds (which it upheld, against an initiative), striking down parental notification for a minor daughter's abortion.[7] Especially in the death penalty reversals, the court experienced a shake-up through the recall elections that ended the tenures of Chief Justice Rose Bird and Associate Justices Joseph Grodin and Cruz Reynoso. Their departure enabled then-governor George Deukmejian to appoint three justices, who, however, did not stay long. The court's previous high reputation among state courts had been shattered, and the effects remain today.

State courts are explicitly bound by Article 6 of the U.S. Constitution to acknowledge the Constitution, and laws and treaties made under it, as "the supreme law of the land." But obviously state courts have their own particular state laws and constitutions to interpret. In California, as in other states, the notion of *independent state grounds* provides for a separate test of state constitutionality that can differ from the federal standard. This notion of a separate constitutionalism, which combines conventional conservative and liberal aspirations, gives the California Supreme Court an unusual significance both within the state and on the national scene. According to former justice Grodin, "Law students and lawyers are slowly coming to understand that if they have what they regard as a constitutional issue, it is their responsibility to look first to the state constitution."[8]

Yet such contrariness—which some commentators would call independence or creativity—should not be unexpected, given the history of the court.[9] As provided for by the California Constitution of 1849, the state's supreme court was to consist of a chief justice and two associate justices elected by the state legislature—or by the people in contested elections—for a term of six years, which was later lengthened to ten years. Early Chief Justice Stephen J. Field, a Democrat, was appointed by Abraham Lincoln to the U.S. Supreme Court in 1863. A veteran of the mines, he would prove to be an intriguing figure who took natural rights seriously as an element of his jurisprudence that emphasized the defense of property rights.[10] Several of his opinions on both the California and U.S. Supreme Courts defended the rights of Chinese immigrants on the basis of the equal protection clause of the Fourteenth Amendment and the federal government's powers in foreign policy. The constitution of 1879 would make the court a chief justice and six associate justices, with twelve-year terms. The legislature could remove judges, including those on the supreme court in certain instances.

Today, the California Supreme Court is still composed of seven justices, who each serve for twelve-year terms. Its formal powers have expanded, and its political character is even more pronounced. The judiciary's formal powers, including those of the supreme court, are described in article 6 of the state constitution. The court has original jurisdiction in a narrow range of cases, and its major impact is as an appellate court, reviewing the state courts of appeal decisions that are appealed to it. The procedure is similar to that of the U.S. Supreme Court, which spends much of its time deciding which cases to hear. The California Constitution requires its supreme court to review all death penalty cases; the court may also review the recommendations of the

Commission on Judicial Performance, a body of various judges and citizens, and of the State Bar of California concerning the removal and suspension of judges and attorneys for misconduct.

Justices are nominated by the governor after their qualifications are reviewed by the State Bar Association's Judicial Nominees Evaluation Commission. Nominees must then be confirmed by the **Commission on Judicial Appointments**. Thus the state legislature is bypassed. The Commission on Judicial Appointments "consists of the Chief Justice, the Attorney General, and the presiding justice of the court of appeal of the affected district . . . or, when a nomination or appointment to the Supreme Court is to be considered, the presiding justice who has presided longest on any court of appeal."[11] If a justice is filling a retiring justice's term, he or she must run for election at the next gubernatorial election for a twelve-year term.

Besides the supreme court, California has two levels of lower courts, superior and appellate. The municipal courts have now been absorbed into superior courts. The consolidation was brought about by yet another example of direct democracy, Proposition 220, in 1998, permitting judges in each county to vote for unification, bringing about greater efficiency in the court system. By February 2001, judges in all fifty-eight counties had voted to unify their trial courts.

Superior Courts

There are currently 2,047 judges, commissioners, referees, assigned judges, and temporary judges in the superior court system.[12] The superior courts are trial courts. All these judges (with the exception of the former municipal court judges) must have been a California attorney or a judge for at least ten years preceding election or appointment. Superior court judges serve six-year terms and are elected by county voters on a nonpartisan ballot at a general election. The governor appoints judges to vacant positions, but they must run for election once that term has expired. Over 80 percent of judges first take their seat on the bench as a result of gubernatorial appointment resulting from a vacancy. **Superior courts** hear *criminal* cases involving infractions, misdemeanors, and felonies, along with the full range of *civil* cases, including divorces, and juvenile cases. Of the 7.7 million cases filed annually, 6.2 million are criminal, most of which involve traffic violations. About nine hundred thousand civil cases are heard in superior courts each year, along with about four hundred thousand cases on family matters. The number of juvenile cases heard annually is approximately one hundred thousand. Probate cases round out the list at about forty thousand cases per year.[13] As for court size, the counties that are smaller in population, like Lassen County, may have only two judges, while Los Angeles County has 465.[14]

Courts of Appeal

The next highest level is the **courts of appeal**, with six districts divided regionally—two in Southern California, two in the Bay Area, one in Sacramento, and another in Fresno—with a total of 105 justices. These courts, which meet in panels of three, are required to handle timely appeals from all the lower courts and from some public agencies, such as the Workers' Compensation Appeal Board, numbering some 20,391 proceedings. The appeals concern broader issues than those of fact, which are settled at the lower court levels. These issues can involve proper trial procedure, correct interpretation of a law or a constitution (California or federal), or proper application of a law. Given this requirement of expertise, the justices hear the cases without a jury and make decisions. About 9 percent of all opinions will be published—those of interest to the broader legal community. Dissatisfied parties may appeal to the California Supreme Court, but that court chooses the appeals cases it hears, other than death penalty cases, which it must hear.[15]

Functions of the Courts

The dramatic function often played by the U.S. Supreme Court—consider controversial Supreme Court decisions from *McCulloch v. Maryland* to *Bush v. Gore*, from *Dred Scott v. Sanford* to *Roe v. Wade*—overshadows these basic functions of courts. As Abraham Lincoln, who was a country lawyer before entering politics, observed, "Judicial decisions have two uses—first, to absolutely determine the case decided, and secondly, to indicate to the public how other similar cases will be decided when they arise. For the latter use, they are called 'precedents' and 'authorities.'"[16] We will consider both roles.

To exemplify the different functions of the courts and the prosecutors, take the example of the infamous O. J. Simpson murder trial. The district attorney for Los Angeles County wanted this criminal case tried by jurors downtown rather than from the opulent Bel Air neighborhood where the murders occurred. This strategy, intended to diffuse racial tensions following a conviction of the African American Simpson, produced an overwhelmingly black pool of jurors. The presiding judge of the superior court insisted on a pretrial hearing for an indictment rather than a grand jury, which, he argued, had been swayed by pretrial publicity. Once the jury declared Simpson innocent, the case could not be appealed because another trial would have meant an unconstitutional double jeopardy. However, he was sued in tort, before another superior court judge, for damages stemming from his actions, was judged at fault, and now owes considerable monetary damages to the victims' families.

Another example of how the different levels of courts operate is provided by the *Bakke* affirmative action case. Allan Bakke, a Marine veteran of Vietnam and a mechanical engineer, chose to become a doctor despite his established career and age of thirty-two when he first applied for the University of California at Davis (UC Davis) Medical School. To make himself competitive for medical school he took undergraduate courses in biology and chemistry. After being turned down twice in 1973 and 1974, Bakke became convinced that the university was admitting applicants far less qualified than he was, solely on the grounds of their race or ethnic origin. The medical school admissions were divided into two different pools: a general applicant pool and a "special admissions" pool of "economically and/or educationally disadvantaged" minorities, from which 16 percent of the entering class would be drawn. None of these were non-Latino whites, and the admission procedures and standards differed dramatically for the two pools. For example, the grade point average for those accepted from the general applicants was 3.5, but that for the special admittees was 2.6. Other dramatic differences were found in standardized test results. In addition, Bakke's test scores placed him well above the average of the general admittee pool.

Bakke's attorney argued before a Yolo County superior court judge that he should be admitted into the medical school and that the UC Davis admissions scheme violated the U.S. Civil Rights Act of 1964 and both the California and U.S. constitutions. The judge agreed with Bakke on the legal and constitutional issues but denied him admission to the medical school. UC Davis, the judge argued, first had to prove they had not discriminated against Bakke. The university appealed to the California Supreme Court. "At the time, the California Supreme Court was perceived as being the most liberal appellate state court in America,"[17] but the court affirmed the superior court judge, 6–1. Justice Stanley Mosk's opinion ordered the superior court judge to determine whether Bakke should be admitted. When the judge would not make that determination, the supreme court ordered Bakke's immediate admission into the medical school.

The U.S. Supreme Court accepted the UC Davis appeal and stayed Bakke's admission, pending its decision on the case. The U.S. Supreme Court split its vote in a complicated 5–4 decision, with two majorities and six opinions, which accepted the U.S. (and implicitly the California) Constitution's Fourteenth Amendment equal protection argument of the California Supreme Court—but not the U.S. Civil Rights Act violation argument. Justice Powell's opinion for the court did not eliminate affirmative action but only those forms that made race or ethnicity decisive for admitting or rejecting an applicant to a program. Thus, he cut back considerably on California Justice Mosk's sweeping constitutional and legal condemnation of racial and ethnic preferences, but he preserved Bakke's right to enter UC Davis Medical School (438 U.S. 265). Subsequently, a California Superior Court later awarded legal fees to Bakke's attorney, payable from the university. In 1982 Bakke, just prior to turning forty-two, graduated from UC Davis medical school. He is currently an M.D. in Minnesota.

The issue of racial and ethnic preferences remains a controversial one in California. Proposition 209, which invalidated preferences by public employers, passed with a 55 percent majority in 1996. A federal judge who attempted to declare it unconstitutional was overruled by the Ninth Circuit Court of Appeals. Judges played a political role throughout the progress of Proposition 209, such as certifying the ballot description of the proposition, which read, "The state shall not discriminate against, or grant preferential treatment to any individual or group, on the basis of race, sex, color ethnicity or national origin in the operation of public employment, public education, or public contracting."[18]

The need for California law to yield to the Supremacy Clause of the U.S. Constitution (article 6, section 2) is vividly illustrated by the U.S. Supreme Court's decision in *United States v. Oakland Cannabis Buyers' Cooperative* (2001). In his Supreme Court opinion, Justice Clarence Thomas declared that federal law does not permit a medical exception to prohibiting the distribution of marijuana. While the decision did not invalidate California's Proposition 215, which permitted the medical use of marijuana, it sets up a clash between state-approved medical marijuana distributors and federal prosecutorial authorities.

The role of the California Supreme Court in checking not just other branches of government but also the initiative process itself is dramatically illustrated by *Raven v. Deukmejian*. In *Raven*, the court ruled unanimously that Proposition 115, which had restricted the independent state grounds doctrine to make California criminal law consistent with federal constitutional interpretation, was unconstitutional: "The Constitution shall not be construed by the courts to afford greater rights to criminal defendants than those afforded by the Constitution of the United States." The court maintained that the proposition was a revision of the California Constitution, not an amendment, and that only the legislature or a constitutional convention, not an initiative, could revise the constitution. This action of the post–Rose Bird court, led by Deukmejian appointee Malcolm Lucas and two other Republican appointees, stunned observers and once more confirmed the activist reputation of the court, regardless of its political composition.

The dispute over so-called same-sex marriage is another example of the role that the courts play in the initiative process. Voters approved a statute initiative in 2000 (Proposition 22) that defined marriage as between a man and a woman. The measure, which clarified California law on this issue, received over 60 percent of the vote. The state supreme court struck down the law in 2008, declaring the ballot proposition unconstitutional. In a close 4–3 decision, the court found that marriage was a fundamental right.[19] Supporters of Proposition 22 took their efforts to the next level by placing a constitutional amendment, which would overrule the supreme court, on the ballot later that same year. In November 2008, a majority of voters supported the amendment (Proposition 8) to define marriage as between a man and a woman. The election results led some in the gay rights movement to protest supporters of Proposition 8. Thousands of gay rights activists protested outside a Mormon temple in Los Angeles, seemingly angered by the support that Proposition 8 received from Mormons. Furthermore, some activists published names and addresses of business owners who supported Proposition 8, in the hopes that those unhappy with the election would boycott the business owners. In one example in Los Angeles, "dozens of gay activists descended on the El Coyote restaurant with signs and placards. They chanted 'Shame on you,' cussed at patrons and began a boycott of the cafe." Apparently, the daughter of the restaurant's owner had donated $100 to the Proposition 8 campaign.[20] The issue then moved to the federal courts, as claimants in favor of same-sex marriage argued that Proposition 8 violated civil rights provisions in the U.S. Constitution. In a limited decision, the U.S. Supreme Court refused to overrule lower federal court rulings that Proposition 8 violated the U.S. Constitution.[21]

In the area of criminal law, California courts may further involve themselves in the constitutionality of "three strikes" legislation, which requires a sentencing judge to impose a penalty of life imprisonment without parole on the third conviction for a crime. Opponents argue that this leads to life terms for stealing a pizza. Proponents point to the increasing numbers of felons leaving California to avoid a third strike and life imprisonment. The three strikes law survived U.S. Supreme Court review, but was subsequently weakened by a ballot initiative in 2012 (Proposition 36).[22]

Finally, among many other examples, we can note *American Academy of Pediatrics v. Lungren*, which interpreted the right to privacy guaranteed by the California Constitution as a result of an initiative passed in 1972. The court declared unconstitutional the 1987 California statute requiring parental consent for a minor to obtain an abortion. The court opinion, written by Chief Justice Ron George, held that California had independent state grounds, separate from the U.S. Constitution, to declare the law unconstitutional. The explicitly guaranteed right of privacy for Californians, whatever the U.S. Supreme Court held, gave its inhabitants the right of abortion, over any other considerations, parental or otherwise.

Issue Highlight for Chapter 8: Three Strikes Law

In 1994, Fresno resident Mike Reynolds and Assemblyman Bill Jones crafted a three strikes proposal and simultaneously submitted it as a ballot initiative and legislative bill. Reynolds's eighteen-year-old daughter was murdered in 1992 by an ex-con with multiple prior convictions. Their efforts met with initial difficulty. The Public Safety Committee in the Democrat-dominated assembly refused to approve the bill, and, despite an immediate burst of support, the initiative petition process became bogged down. The brutal murder and kidnapping of Polly Klaas changed the political landscape.

The three strikes law was enacted by the legislature and signed by Governor Pete Wilson on March 7, 1994. AB 971 was passed as an urgency measure—requiring a two-thirds majority in each chamber—due, in large part, to the popularity of the impending statutory initiative proposal that eventually was passed as Proposition 184 in November 1994 with 72 percent support.[23]

Under this law, the first two strikes must be serious or violent felonies, but a third strike could be triggered by any felony. A second-strike conviction carried double the normal sentence, and a third-strike conviction mandated a sentence of twenty-five years to life. Critics of the law decried the fact that felons had been given sentences of twenty-five years to life for stealing a slice of pizza, a bottle of vitamins, videotapes, and other seemingly minor crimes. Supporters of the law pointed out that in each of these "horror" stories, the seemingly minor offense was the last in a long series of crimes. Every third striker had previously committed at least two serious or violent felonies.

In 2003, the U.S. Supreme Court upheld California's three strikes law. Although there was no majority opinion in *Ewing v. California*, five members of the court rejected the challenge that the California law violated the cruel and unusual punishment clause of the Eighth Amendment to the U.S. Constitution. In 2004, the voters of California rejected Proposition 66, a ballot initiative that sought to weaken the three strikes law by a 57–43 margin. In 2012, however, voters reversed course and overwhelmingly approved a weakening of the three strikes law by a 61–39 margin. As a result of Proposition 36, a third strike triggers a life sentence only if the crime was serious or violent.

Conclusion

The California court system, headed by its supreme court, gives the California Constitution much of its meaning. But the dramatic decisions made by the supreme court should not overshadow the work of the civil and criminal trial courts and the courts of appeal, which interpret and apply the law in specific cases. The use of independent state grounds by the California Supreme Court has led to battles over the court's legitimate power; despite an initiative (Proposition 115) restricting its powers in a specific area, the court declared it unconstitutional. Whether the supreme court can unilaterally shape public policy in controversial areas is highly disputed, as its decisions concerning affirmative action, abortion, and criminal law demonstrate.

9

The Budget and Government Finance

"How is it," I asked, "that you do not put a fee on spirits?" "Our legislators have indeed often thought of it," he replied, "but the undertaking is difficult. A revolt is feared; and besides, the members who voted such a law would be very sure of not being reelected."[1]

BUDGETS ARE MORE THAN mere accounting tools. In the modern administrative state, they have become the chief means by which policies are implemented. The rise of budget politics since the advent of the Progressive era poses a serious challenge to the survival of our republican form of government. Budget rhetoric tends to swirl around complicated jargon and technical terminology. The ability of citizens to accurately assess the actions of their representatives becomes less certain. What is the meaning of a representative's vote on a massive budget bill, one that contains thousands of individual expenditure and tax items? Many expenditure and taxation items are enacted with little fanfare. However, these same items can have a profound and lasting impact on the ability of citizens to protect their natural rights to life, liberty, and the pursuit of happiness.[2]

Budget Process

Each year, the governor is required to submit a balanced budget to the legislature by January 10.[3] The governor sets the overall policy direction of the proposed budget, as state agencies are required to provide their budget requests and any other necessary information to the governor. State agencies and departments cannot send direct budget requests to the legislature, but must work through a cabinet agency, the **Department of Finance (DOF)**. The DOF acts as a clearinghouse for the budget requests of state agencies and departments.[4]

Anticipating economic conditions is crucial in the preparation of a successful budget proposal. Economic downturns can cause a decline in the growth of tax revenues and have the potential to cause budget deficits, which are prohibited by both the California Code and Constitution. An accurate economic forecast will provide the governor and the legislature with a good estimate as to the prudent levels of proposed taxing and spending.

The budget proposal is submitted in the form of a bill, which contains itemized expenditures and the anticipated means of payment for each. The governor's proposal is usually outlined in the annual State of the State address. This announcement is one of the major policy events in the legislative year. The bill is then officially introduced into each chamber of the legislature by the house and senate budget committees. Before the committees take any further action, the **Legislative Analyst's Office (LAO)** conducts a thorough examination of the budget. The LAO is a nonpartisan organization of policy experts selected by both chambers of the legislature; it assesses the strengths and weaknesses of the governor's proposals. Items that frequently receive close scrutiny by the LAO are the accuracy of the economic forecasts, the level and type of proposed spending, and tax levels. The LAO report is usually completed by the end of February.[5]

At this time, the senate and assembly budget committees begin holding a series of separate hearings. Key participants in these hearings are members of state agencies and departments, as well as lobbyists. The purpose of these hearings is to provide members of the committees with enough information to make the best possible decision. Once the hearings are concluded, each committee produces a proposed budget that is sent to the floor of each chamber for consideration. The two documents are almost never identical. Therefore, at this stage, there are three separate budget proposals: the governor's, the assembly's, and the senate's. The final outcome will be a compromise among the three documents.

The next major step in the process is the governor's May Revision, which includes any adjustments to the original proposal that might have been necessary due to unforeseen circumstances. The budget bill in each chamber must be approved by a majority vote of each chamber. Prior to the passage of Proposition 25 (2010), a two-thirds vote was required in each chamber to pass a budget—twenty-seven out of forty in the senate and fifty-four out of eighty in the assembly. This requirement was one of the distinguishing features of California government. Since a majority party rarely attains such margins in any legislature, the two-thirds requirement allowed the minority party a vital role in the budget process. In fact, the minority leaders of each chamber were so important to the process that they—along with the governor, speaker of the assembly, and the president pro tempore of the senate—were known as the Big Five. With the passage of Proposition 25, the role of the minority party in the budget process is diminished, although not eliminated. Tax increases must still be approved by a two-thirds vote.

Once each chamber produces its version of the budget, a conference committee is convened to reconcile the differences. The conference committee is formed by members from both chambers. Once the conference committee produces a single compromise budget, the document is sent back to each chamber. This compromise budget is sent to the governor on a majority vote of each legislative chamber. Like the governor's proposed budget, the budget produced by the legislature must be balanced.[6] After receiving the legislative budget, the governor has the option of reducing or eliminating any spending measure by exercising a line item veto. Like other vetoes, this is subject to override as well, by a two-thirds vote of each legislative chamber.

The legislature must complete its work by June 15 for the budget to be in place for the start of the new fiscal year, which begins on July 1. When the requirement for legislative approval was a two-thirds vote in each chamber, the deadline was rarely met. It was common for the budget process to move well into August or September. With the passage of Proposition 25 and the institution of a majority-vote rule on budgets, budgets will have a better chance of being approved by the June 15 deadline.

Revenues and Expenditures

The process just described refers to the **general fund budget**, the law that authorizes annual spending and taxing. However, three other categories of revenues and expenditures are not taken into consideration in the general fund budget: special funds, federal funds, and bond issues. **Special funds** are revenues that are automatically spent on specific areas, such as motor vehicle–related taxes and fees that must be spent on transportation. **Federal funds** consist of grants made by the federal government to the state to carry out particular programs. Special funds and federal funds are, for the most part, beyond the ability of the legislature and governor to control. The **bond fund** is not part of the general fund budget due to the unique characteristics of the projects that are in this category. Bond funds, which will be discussed in more detail later in this chapter, are for long-term capital projects that do not fit into the time frame of an annual general fund budget.

One needs to be cognizant of these different budgets, because of their size. For the 2013–2014 fiscal year, the entire budget—which includes the general fund, special funds, bond funds, and federal funds—was $232.9 billion. Of this, the general fund accounted for $96.2 billion, special funds for $42 billion, bond funds for $7 billion, and federal funds for $87.6 billion.[7]

General Fund Expenditures

For the 2013–2014 fiscal year, the overwhelming portion of state general fund spending was in the areas of K–12 education, health and human services, higher education, and prisons. Spending on K–12 education accounted for 41.2 percent of all expenditures. Health and human services accounted for 29.17 percent. Higher education took up 11.3 percent. Prison expenditures were 9.25 percent of the budget. When we combine these three areas, we see that about 91.45 cents out of every general fund dollar spent by the state of California is made on teaching students, helping the needy, and incarcerating criminals. Thus, when budget cuts are enacted, it is no surprise that these areas are affected most deeply. It would be impossible to enact meaningful budget reform without addressing these categories of spending.[8]

Overall Revenues

The money to pay for general fund expenditures comes from a variety of sources. However, the two main methods of collecting state revenue consist of the personal income tax and the sales tax. For the 2013–2014 fiscal year, the income tax provided 62.6 percent of general fund state revenues, and the sales tax accounted for 23.7 percent. These two areas represent well over three-fourths of all state revenues. The next two biggest sources of revenue are corporate taxes (8.7 percent) and insurance taxes (2.20 percent).[9]

Characteristics of Each Tax

A tax can be either a **progressive tax** or a **regressive tax,** depending on the relative burden it places on those who pay it. A tax is considered progressive if the rate of taxation increases as income rises. It is considered regressive if this relative rate decreases as income rises, placing a heavier relative burden on those with less income.

Keep in mind that a tax rate is different from the amount of tax collected. For example, assume that California imposed a 100 percent tax rate on all personal income. If one made $50,000 a year, one would pay $50,000 in taxes. What is your best guess as to the amount of revenue the state of California would actually receive? If you guessed $0, you are probably correct. At a 100 percent tax rate, an individual with a full-time job would take home the same amount of money as a person who did not work. Let us assume that the voters became angered over the imposition of such a ridiculous tax and elected new representatives who reduced the rate to 5 percent. What would the state revenues then be? It is hard to estimate, but one could easily imagine that there would be an increased incentive to work. This would allow the state to collect 5 percent of the income. Therefore, at a lower tax rate the state would collect a greater amount of tax dollars.[10] Let us now examine the characteristics of each of the major categories of taxation in California.

Income Tax

The California income tax is progressive, which means that the rate of taxation increases as one is better able to pay the tax and is quite sensitive to the relative financial condition of a taxpayer. The progression of the income tax can be illustrated by the relative tax burdens of people at different income levels.[11] According to a study provided by the LAO, taxpayers with incomes of over $200,000 a year pay approximately 55 percent of all income taxes, even though they comprise only 5 percent of all income tax returns. On the other hand, taxpayers with under $50,000 in annual income pay less than 6 percent of all income taxes, even though they comprise nearly 45 percent of all returns.[12] Furthermore, California's income taxes are indexed to match inflation rates, so that a taxpayer is not pushed into a higher rate bracket simply because wages have kept up with the rise in prices. However, these characteristics make the level of tax revenue collected by the state heavily reliant on the condition of the economy. During periods of economic growth, the level of income tax revenue increases, but in downturns, the level of revenue falls. Why does the state continue to rely so heavily on the income tax? The answer is that the income tax is a convenient financial instrument for the state because of payroll deduction. It is easy to administer.

Sales Tax

Unlike the income tax, the sales tax is regressive by nature. Everyone, regardless of income, needs to purchase a basic level of food, clothes, and transportation. Those with less money find themselves in the position of paying a larger portion of their income on these necessities. Therefore, taxes on the sales of these items will disproportionately impact those with smaller incomes. However, measures can be taken to mitigate the regressiveness of sales taxes, such as the exemption of food items.

Fees, Item-Specific Taxes, and Property Taxes

In addition to the income and sales taxes, a variety of taxes and fees are peculiar to a particular product. A gasoline tax is perhaps the most regressive tax. One must pay the required rate per gallon regardless of income. The annual automobile registration fee, on the other hand, is indirectly progressive because it is tied to the value of one's automobile. As long as one purchases an automobile that corresponds with his or her income level, then the ability to pay is treated progressively. What about so-called sin taxes on tobacco and alcohol? The effective tax rate could be seen as regressive, but these items are not necessities, and a consumer has a great deal of choice over whether to use these products and, thereby, pay the tax associated with them. The same would apply to park fees and fishing licenses.

Property taxes, as mentioned previously, are a revenue mainstay of local governments in the United States (which are discussed in greater detail in chapter 10). In one sense, the property tax is indirectly linked with income because one pays a larger amount of property taxes on a home worth $800,000 than on one worth $300,000. Assuming that people match the purchase price of a home to their income, it can be said that property taxes are progressive. However, the regressive nature of the property tax comes to the fore due to its unresponsiveness to changes in the homeowner's income. The property tax must be paid regardless of whether one is still employed; otherwise, a government may take possession of the home and sell it to collect the required revenue.

Furthermore, one could face an increasing tax burden even when one is prospering in an occupation. If home values suddenly rise at enormous rates, the property tax could become a significant financial burden. A situation like this arose in California during the 1970s. To remedy it, Proposition 13, a measure that limited the increase in property taxes, was approved by voters in 1978. Proposition 13 is just one of a number of influential ballot initiatives in the area of government revenues and expenditures. It is discussed in more detail later and in chapter 10.

Ballot Initiatives

Proposition 13, which was passed in 1978, limits general property tax rates to 1 percent of assessed value and limits the increase in assessed value after a property is purchased or built. Proposition 4, passed in 1979, limits the growth of state spending from year to year by either the inflation rate or population growth. Propositions 6 and 7 were approved in 1982 to limit inheritance taxes and require the indexing of income tax rates, respectively.

Passed in 1984, Proposition 37 allowed for the creation of a state lottery, with the stipulation that a certain portion of the funds be earmarked for education. Propositions 62 (1986) and 218 (1996) place strict limits on the ability of local governments to raise taxes. Proposition 98 was passed in 1988 and requires that at least 40 percent of the general fund budget be devoted to K–12 and community college education. Propositions 99 (1988) and 10 (1998) imposed a surtax on cigarettes and other tobacco products, with the stipulation that these funds be earmarked for health programs.

The sales tax on food items, including snacks and bottled water, was repealed after the passage of Proposition 163 in 1992. In the same year, voters decided to increase sales taxes by one-half of a cent, with the requirement that the funds be used to support police and fire departments. Proposition 39 (2000) rolled back some of the property tax limits put in place by Proposition 13. Proposition 25 (2010) reduced the legislative majority necessary to pass a budget from a two-thirds super majority in each chamber to a simple majority. Proposition 30 (2012) increased income and sales taxes to avoid cuts to key public services. Proposition 2 (2014) required that the government set aside a portion of tax revenues in a "rainy day account," in anticipation of future budget crises.

Bonds

A **bond** is a certificate that is issued by a government and purchased by individuals or institutions, and major capital projects are supported out of the bond fund. These projects often require several years of construction and entail large initial costs and, therefore, are not well suited for annual evaluation in the general fund budget process. At a stipulated future date, the government agrees to repay the cost of the certificate, along with a prearranged level of interest. There are three main types of bonds: general obligation bonds, revenue bonds, and special assessment bonds.

General obligation bonds are repaid by a government from its current revenues. For these bonds to be issued by the state, each chamber of the legislature must approve them by a two-thirds vote. In addition, they must be approved by a majority of voters. At the local level, most general obligation bonds require majority approval by the legislature of the jurisdiction in question, along with two-thirds support of the voters.

Revenue bonds are repaid by the money generated from the project itself, such as airports and toll roads. Revenue bonds only require a majority vote by the jurisdiction's legislature. *Special assessment bonds* are used by local governments and are paid by assessing property owners according to their relative use of the service provided. These bonds must be approved by a majority of the local legislature, along with votes from owners of a majority of the property that would be affected.

Several firms have established bond rating systems, which are like a person's credit rating, for state and local governments. These systems reflect an entity's history of fulfilling financial obligations. The higher the bond rating, the more confidence a purchaser has that the government will pay the agreed-on principal and interest by the required date.[13]

Issue Highlight for Chapter 9: California's Budget Drama

When Governor Jerry Brown took office in 2011, he inherited a $26 billion budget deficit. The Great Recession is partly to blame for this. About 80 percent of state revenues come from the income and sales taxes. In bad economic times, these revenue sources plummet. The structural problems with the California budget, however, go well beyond falling revenues in a downward economic cycle. California's budget woes were present before the economic crash of 2008. Former Governor Gray Davis was recalled from office in 2003, largely as a result of public discontent over budget deficits. Arnold Schwarzenegger was then placed in office with a mandate to fix the problem. He failed, as did the Democrat-controlled legislature. Governor Brown was elected with the same mandate. He faced a daunting challenge.[14]

For more than a decade, California had lived beyond its means. Some observers point out that Governor Brown helped create the problem during his first stint as governor (1975–1983) when he approved collective bargaining for state employees. Through labor union agreements, state employees have been able to negotiate higher salary and benefit packages.[15] Other analysts place blame on Proposition 13 (1978), which dramatically reduced property taxes. The state was then left to rely heavily on volatile income and sales tax revenues.[16] Another cause of our chronic deficits could be a complicated budget process, which encouraged stalemate. Rather than solve the problem, California public officials over the past ten years would "kick-the-can-down-the-road" and hope for a dramatic economic recovery and, perhaps, additional help from the federal government.[17]

Whatever the cause, the fact remained that California had a chronic spending problem. From 1990 to 2009, tax revenues to the state increased 167 percent. If spending would have remained steady with the rate of inflation, about 4 percent per year, the state would have had a $15 billion budget surplus. Instead, state spending rose 181 percent.[18] Accordingly, state budgets were out of balance before the Great Recession struck in 2008. With the onset of the economic downturn, a chronic problem turned into a crisis.

Upon taking office in 2011, Governor Brown submitted a series of dramatic cuts to welfare programs and higher education, "For 10 years we've had budget gimmicks and tricks that pushed us deep into debt. We must now return California to fiscal responsibility and get our state on the road to economic recovery."[19] The governor's plan to balance the budget was based on the assumption that the proposed spending cuts would induce tax weary Californians to approve an extension of tax increases. Brown's gamble paid off, so to speak. Voters approved Proposition 30 in 2012 by a margin of 55–45 percent. Furthermore, voters approved the creation of a budget "rainy day" fund through Proposition 2 (2014) by a massive margin of 69–31 percent.

While these measures may address the deficit in the short run, there is concern that further tax increases could make California even more unfriendly to businesses.[20] In addition, future state pension obligations could crowd out state spending for key government functions. This raises the larger question of the proper balance between adequate public spending—to provide good roads, schools, and crime control—and lower taxes and less-burdensome regulations, which attract businesses to the state. There is no easy answer to this question, especially in California.

Conclusion

The governor is required to submit a budget to the legislature by January 10, and this proposal is usually outlined in the annual State of the State address. The legislature is required to send its version of the budget back to the governor by June 15, but this deadline has been rarely met. The largest areas of spending are education and welfare and the two largest categories of taxation are the income tax and the sales tax. Large capital projects are not funded out of the general fund budget; instead, bonds support these projects. There are three main types of bonds: general obligation bonds, revenue bonds, and special assessment bonds. Several firms have established bond-rating systems, which are like credit ratings, for state and local governments.

10

Local Government

A very civilized society tolerates only with difficulty the trials of freedom in a township; it is revolted at the sight of its numerous lapses and despairs of success before having attained the final result of experience.

Thus as long as township freedom has not entered into mores, it is easy to destroy it, and it can enter into mores only after having subsisted for a long time in the laws.[1]

TOCQUEVILLE BELIEVED THAT he had discovered the essence of democracy in America. The ghost in the American machine was the principle of equality. It was everywhere and nowhere, moving through a myriad of political institutions: "The laws differ and their outward features change, but the same spirit animates them."[2] This spirit had no less a goal than the leveling of all differences, especially those of opinion. This would lead to the development of a centralized administration that would implement a "soft despotism" in the United States.

One of the potential bulwarks against the rising tide of soft despotism was local self-government. From his observations of New England town meetings, Tocqueville argued that a certain degree of local autonomy helped to foster a spirit of civic duty. When considering matters of local government, citizens could more easily notice that their immediate welfare was intimately tied to the welfare of the community. Visceral self-interest could be, in this way, transformed into a **self-interest rightly understood**. If this spirit were to become predominant, America might avoid being dominated by a democratic centralized administration.

If Tocqueville were to examine the condition of local government in California today, he would find that local government in California is a maze of cities, counties, **regional associations,** local agency formation commissions, school districts, and **special districts.**

Cities

There are 482 cities in California, and they have primary or shared responsibility for implementing policies in the following areas: police, fire, streets, sewage, storm drainage, sanitation, planning, and zoning. According to state law, there are two basic types of cities: general law cities and charter cities. A **general law city** is governed according to specific provisions in the California Code, and a **charter city** has more flexibility in its management of administrative and fiscal affairs. There are 121 charter cities in California, with the rest being general law cities.[3]

The city council is the basic institution of government for California cities. City councils contain at least five members, elected to staggered four-year terms, and their elections can be based on either the ward system or the at-large system. The ward system operates much like elections to the California legislature, with council members being elected from single-member districts (wards) within the city. On the other hand, council members in an at-large system do not represent a specific district within the city. Instead, new council members are chosen by voters in a citywide election. For example, if a city council were to have two of its five seats up for election, the top two candidates in a citywide election would serve on the council, regardless of the neighborhood in which they lived.[4]

Mayors can be directly elected by the city at large or selected by the council from among its members. A mayoral position can be either weak or strong: Strong mayors have extensive powers to hire and fire city officials, and weak mayors lack these powers but fulfill a ceremonial role. All but the largest cities, which include Los Angeles and San Francisco, employ a city manager as the *chief municipal administrative officer.* The job of the city manager is to run a city's day-to-day operations and monitor its finances. Since the city manager serves at the pleasure of the city council, his or her level of flexibility is a barometer of the balance of power between a mayor and a city council. Weak-mayor cities are often called *council/manager governments*, and strong-mayor cities are referred to as *mayor/council governments.*[5]

A sample of the variety of California city governments is displayed in table 10.1. Each city is compared according to (1) whether the city has a charter, (2) its method of electing a city council, (3) the strength of the office of mayor,

TABLE 10.1
Comparative Government of Selected California Cities

City	Population	Mayor	Election	Charter	City Manager
Los Angeles	3,884,307	Strong	Ward	Yes	No
San Bernardino	213, 708	Strong	Ward	Yes	Yes
Petaluma	59,440	Weak	At-large	Yes	Yes
Crescent City	7,188	Weak	At-large	No	Yes

Sources: Population of Los Angeles, San Bernardino, Petaluma, and Crescent City, U.S. Census Bureau, http://factfinder.census.gov; City of Los Angeles, http://cityclerk.lacity.org/cps/pdf/govtglnc.pdf; City of San Bernardino, http://www.ci.san-bernardino.ca.us/cityhall/default.asp; City Government, Petaluma, http://cityofpetaluma.net/cclerk/faq.html; Crescent City Government, http://www.crescentcity.org/citycouncil.html (all sites accessed February 1, 2015).

and (4) whether there is a city manager that has principal responsibility for running city operations. Los Angeles is at one extreme with a mayor/council form of government, while the harbor town of Crescent City in Del Norte County is the quintessential council/manager city. All of these cities selected have charters except for Crescent City, the smallest, which is a general law city. The two largest cities in the sample, Los Angeles and San Bernardino, elect city council members by means of a ward system. The two smallest, Petaluma and Crescent City, elect council members through the at-large method. As for the strength of the mayor's office in each city, Los Angeles and San Bernardino have strong-mayor systems. Petaluma and Crescent City leave most of the executive decision making to a council-appointed city manager. As stated earlier, this sample reflects the general condition of California city government: the smaller the city, the more likely it is to be ruled by a city council, which is elected in an at-large manner.

At-large elections and the employment of city managers are institutions dating from the Progressive era (1880s–1920s). The goal of Progressivism, led in California by Governor Hiram Johnson (1911–1917), was to end the patronage style of governments instituted by large-city political machines. The spoils system was to be replaced with a more rational bureaucratic style of rule.

Counties

There are fifty-eight counties in California; each county is a legal entity of the State of California and is governed by a five-member board of supervisors. Most of the counties elect their supervisors by means of a single-member district system similar to that of the ward system in city government. The primary areas of policy responsibility for counties are public health, public records, sanitation, sheriff's department, and welfare.

For the most part, county policy responsibilities, including the costs of running the court system, are mandated by the state or federal government. In addition, some counties have contracts with local governments within their jurisdiction to share the costs for certain services. This is called the Lakewood Plan, after the California city that initially adopted this method of providing services. The most common policy areas that fall under the Lakewood Plan are fire and police services.[6]

Most counties in California belong to regional associations. These organizations are quasi-governmental units devoted to cooperation and discussion on issues of regional concern, with mass transit being a prominent example. Counties within a regional association send representatives to serve on a board of directors, share research data, conduct studies, and resolve inter-county disputes. The two largest associations are the Southern California Association of Governments and the Association of Bay Area Governments. The Southern California association is formed by representatives from Imperial, Los Angeles, Orange, Riverside, San Bernardino, and Ventura counties. The Bay Area group consists of representatives from Alameda, Contra Costa, Marin, Napa, San Francisco, San Mateo, Santa Clara, and Solano counties.

Special Districts and School Districts

The first special districts in California were created over a hundred years ago to deal with irrigation.[7] In 1900, there were over fifty irrigation districts throughout the state. Since then, the number and variety of special districts have grown considerably. There are 2,765 special district governments in California; included in this are 473 natural resources districts, 353 fire districts, 70 housing and community development districts, and remaining miscellaneous districts that include such things as airports, sanitation, and mosquito control. State legislation allows for the creation of special districts, which are charged with jurisdiction over a specific area of policy and granted carefully enumerated powers. However, while a special district government is limited in its scope, it is still a *government* having the power to tax and enforce regulations.[8]

There are 1,044 school districts in California.[9] The local government body of a school district is the school board, and the board's chief executive officer is the superintendent. The relationship of the superintendent to the school board is much like that of the city manager to the city council. Voters elect members of the school board who, in turn, appoint a superintendent to administer the district.

Proposition 13

Housing values in California during the early 1970s skyrocketed, causing a dramatic increase in property taxes. The successful passage of Proposition 13 in 1978 led to the rollback of property taxes to 1975 levels, set a rate ceiling at 1 percent of assessed valuation, and limited any potential increase in the tax rate to 2 percent a year. In addition, most new local taxes beyond the property tax restrictions in Proposition 13 can only be passed by two-thirds of the voters in the jurisdiction in question.

The debate over Proposition 13 still rages. Those who oppose the measure argue that before Proposition 13 went into effect, local public services in California were the envy of the nation.[10] After the measure's enactment, opponents argue, California's public services are now among the worst. In addition, and perhaps most disturbingly to the opponents, the fiscal relationships between state and local governments are now so complex that it is beyond the understanding of all but the most elite policy analysts. This, the opponents argue, is a threat to the very nature of democratic government. Lastly, opponents argue that the limit on property tax revenue encourages cities to favor retail development instead of residential development because the cities will harvest more sales tax dollars, which are not under the strict limits of Proposition 13. In the end, this could drive up property costs.

According to the supporters of Proposition 13, the most fundamental lesson to be learned from this controversy is not the level of taxation alone but also the very nature of the property tax itself.[11] First, property tax is one of the most regressive taxes because it is not tied to a person's ability to pay. The homeowner must pay the same amount, or even a higher amount, whether or not the person received a raise, took a pay cut, or lost a job. Second, the property tax is difficult to administer. California counties are in charge of property assessment, and as part of this responsibility, they must provide for an assessment appeals process in the likely event of disputes over assessed value. Lastly, the property tax provides a perverse disincentive to homeowners who decide not to improve their property for fear of an increased assessment.

In addition to Proposition 13, other ballot initiatives affecting local government finance have gained majority support and been implemented. Among the most significant are Propositions 62 and 218. Proposition 62 was passed in 1986 and mandated that, in addition to an increase in special taxes, any increase in general taxes must be approved by the voters in that jurisdiction. Proposition 218, which was approved in 1996, extended the provisions of Proposition 62 to charter cities. One ballot initiative, however, modified the terms of Proposition 13 by lowering the two-thirds majority requirement for

school bond measures. Proposition 39 (2000) reduced the supermajority necessary in a school district bond election to 55 percent of the vote.[12]

Issue Highlight for Chapter 10: Special Districts in California

The sheer amount and variety of California's local governments is breath-
taking. Setting aside any notions of civic participation for the time being, a
California citizen would achieve no small feat by simply locating all of the
different units of local government that exercise authority in a given area,
for "every citizen in the state is a resident of a dozen or more units of local
government."[13] There are 4,344 units of local government in California.[14]
To further confuse matters, most of these units do not conform to a commonsense geography. It is possible that "two neighbors might be in the same
transit district but in different water districts, housing districts, and economic
development districts."[15] As opposed to city or county limits that are marked
by road signs, the boundaries of special districts are not obvious to passersby.
Locating and charting the special districts that have jurisdiction over one's
life and property is a daunting task. And even if one did have a professional
background in political geography and were able to identify and draw the
boundaries for all of the governments in one's area, there is no guarantee that
the results of one's labors would provide a clearer picture. It is common for
the boundaries of local governments to "have irregular and uneven boundaries and take on a 'Swiss Cheese' design."[16]

The most strident critics of the tangled web of local government are public
administration theorists, who argue from the perspective of Progressivist
administrative rationality. They state that fragmentation reduces public accountability and causes a lack of coordination that leads to an inefficient administration; therefore, unless the array of local governments is consolidated
into a coherent hierarchy, effective and efficient representative government
at the local level is impossible.[17]

The most strident supporters of the proliferation of local government
units are connected to the public choice (free market) school of economics and have been influenced, in one form or another, by Charles Tiebout.[18]
Contrary to the fears of the administrative rationalists, Tiebout argues that
citizens would receive more efficient and effective service if there were few (if
any) restrictions placed on the increase of local government units in a state.
Local governments would compete with one another for residents and have
incentives to achieve a competitive equilibrium between taxes and services.
When units of government grow too large, they become disconnected with
the citizens who are their customers in the market for public services. The

public choice theorists argue that large consolidated governments create a diseconomy of scale that is likely to produce goal displacement within government bureaucracies.[19]

What about the charge by the administrative rationalists that fragmentation makes democratic accountability nearly impossible? Robert Hawkins argued that there is more than one way to evaluate the level of accountability in a government system.[20] In one sense, it is true that voter turnout in special district elections is low and that citizen participation in the decisions of special districts is limited. However, citizen satisfaction in the quality of services performed by local governments is high, and "[c]itizens living in smaller communities consistently had higher levels of satisfaction with local government services than those living in large communities."[21] According to Hawkins, this "pattern held for schools, street maintenance, police protection, zoning, and parks and recreation."[22] Therefore, if we assume that the citizen is best understood as a consumer of government-provided goods, then the best thing to do about the intricate web of California local government services is to increase their number and level of specialization. On the other hand, if we think more of our citizens than this, perhaps we should be concerned with the tangled web of local government in California.

Conclusion

Alexis de Tocqueville thought that citizen participation in local government was vital to the health of American democracy.[23] If Tocqueville were alive today, he would find a multilayered system of local government in California. The various types of local government in California include counties, cities, special districts, and school districts. Local government finance has been controversial in California. The debate continues over the long-term impact of Proposition 13, which passed in 1978 and dramatically reduced property tax levels in California.

Epilogue

Recall, Return, and Beyond

IN 2003, POLITICAL OBSERVERS across the world focused their attention on California. The nation's most populous state was undergoing a political upheaval. The California state budget was in crisis. Public opinion toward the incumbent governor, Gray Davis, was overwhelmingly unfavorable. Granted, this is not all that uncommon. States go through tough times. Budgets sometimes become unbalanced. Incumbent politicians lose support as a result. What made California's agony such a spectacle, however, was the recall election.

A recall election, in and of itself, is dramatic. Prior to Gray Davis, only one other governor in American history had been recalled. But this kind of drama is one customarily appreciated by scholars of state and local politics, not the general public. Recalls alone are not the stuff of national media events. What made the California recall a worldwide event was what makes so many other things in California the object of public fascination: celebrities, sex, and the courts.

In July 2003, recall supporters had collected enough signatures to put the measure on the ballot in October. The brief campaign would turn out to be one of the strangest and most exciting elections in American history. The writing was on the wall for Gray Davis. It was clear that if the election were allowed to go forward, he would most likely lose. His campaign filed a series of lawsuits challenging the constitutionality of the recall election. These results were unsuccessful.

The campaign to unseat Gray Davis took on a circus atmosphere. Vanity candidates—a controversial journalist, a Green Party environmentalist, entertainers, a former child actor, a pornographer, and over 130 other attention-seekers stepped forward as candidates. In addition, there were three mainstream candidates in the recall election, Lieutenant Governor Cruz Bustamante and state senator Tom McClintock, a conservative Republican. The most prominent candidate, however, was Hollywood megastar Arnold Schwarzenegger who announced his candidacy as a Republican on the *Tonight Show with Jay Leno*.

As the whirlwind campaign drew to a close, it appeared that Schwarzenegger's *Total Recall* would become a reality. He was cruising to victory, with strong polling numbers. But less than a week before the election the *Los Angeles Times* published a story citing anonymous victims claiming Schwarzenegger had groped them. The timing and credibility of the stories were heavily criticized, as many observers thought the *Times* was pushing its political agenda through its news stories. Despite this last-minute controversy, the recall won 55–45 percent and Gray Davis was removed from office. On the second part of the ballot for replacement candidates, Schwarzenegger took 49 percent of the vote, Bustamante 32 percent, and fellow Republican McClintock 13 percent. Arnold Schwarzenegger became governor of the nation's most populous state.

Although he went on to win another term in 2006 against a weak Democrat challenger, his tenure as governor failed to live up to the promise of the 2003 recall movement. Despite his desire to reform California's heavily regulated and bureaucratic political system, his blunt tactics—appearing to pick on teachers, firefighters, and police officers in the 2005 special election—and the efforts of an entrenched Democratic majority in the legislature led to years of stalemate and continued budget deficits. The onset of the Great Recession in 2008 made a bad situation even worse. Unable to run again in 2010 because of term limits, it was *Back to the Future* for the Hollywood-star-turned-would-be-reformer. His poll numbers upon leaving office, driven by massive budget deficits and double-digit unemployment, were as weak as those of Gray Davis in the midst of the recall frenzy.

In 2010, California voters put the state on a path that was no less startling than 2003, but this time without the same level of celebrity sizzle. While much of the rest of the country turned in a more conservative direction—the Republicans made big gains across all levels of government—California Democrats achieved historic political victories, by impressive margins. The red Republican wave sweeping the country crashed at the California border. Blue California got even bluer. Democrats held onto their strong majorities in both chambers of the legislature. Democrats swept the statewide executive elections. Not a single Republican held an elected executive position in the Golden State as a result of the 2010 election, a trend that continues today. Furthermore, one of the most iconic liberal politicians in American history, Jerry Brown, was elected governor. In 2014, Governor Brown was reelected by a wide margin, once again with no Republicans winning any statewide office, in spite of the GOP's strong performance nationwide. This is an amazing change of direction, not only in light of national trends, but also in light of the political mood surrounding the recall election of 2003.

How California fares in the years after the 2014 election will provide a major lesson for political and fiscal analysts, not only here in California but across the nation as well. While many other states and the national government headed in a more conservative direction, California headed in a more liberal direction. If the Democratic leadership of California continues to successfully guide the state out of its fiscal and economic crisis, then liberals across America could claim an important victory for their ideas. On the other hand, if California slides back into fiscal and economic turmoil, there will be no shortage of conservative commentators who will point to our state as a model for others of what not to do: profligate public spending, burdensome regulation, high taxes. The stakes are high and the game has yet to be decided.

In 1835, Tocqueville gazed into the mysterious future for our country and saw both peril and promise. What would this strange new phenomenon of democracy bring forth? The replacement of Arnold Schwarzenegger with the career politician Jerry Brown has taken our state onto a new path. The current economic crisis is, arguably, the biggest challenge this state has faced in a century. With that in mind, we close our discussion of California as Tocqueville closed his great work, *Democracy in America*. We know not whether the great adventure that is democracy in California will lead to "servitude or freedom, to enlightenment or barbarism, to prosperity or misery."[1]

Glossary

attention cycle The level of attention given to a political issue from beginning to end; the public rarely follows an issue with consistent intensity over an extended period of time.

bias The extent to which a sample fails to accurately measure the opinion of the population.

bond A certificate issued by a government to fund major capital projects.

bond funds The pool of money by which capital projects receive financial support.

bureaucracy A hierarchical organization with the stated goal of hiring on the basis of merit.

California Constitutions of 1849 and 1879 The prestatehood constitution of 1849 emphasized the protection of individual rights and limited government; in contrast, the constitutional convention of 1878–1879 produced the California Constitution of 1879, which permitted extensive regulation of economic activity and contained an anti-Chinese article.

centralization Increased governmental power to include the steadfast gaze of a central authority on the details of everyday political and social life. Tocqueville predicted that the United States would develop a growing administrative centralization, and Progressivism brought it to reality.

charter city A city that has greater autonomy to create its own policies.

Chinese immigration Chinese who immigrated to work in early California as laborers and who accounted for approximately 8 percent of the population.

Commission on Judicial Appointments This three-member body consists of the chief justice, the attorney general, and the presiding justice of the court of appeal of the affected district (or, for supreme court nominations, the longest-serving justice on any court of appeal). The governor nominates judges and justices, who then face confirmation by this commission.

Compromise of 1850 Created by the leading statesmen of the time, this set of laws provided for California's entry into the Union as a free state; the possibility of forming slave states out of western territories; the abolition of the slave trade in Washington, D.C.; and the passage of federal fugitive slave laws that provided for the return of escaped slaves to their masters.

court of appeals Panels of justices that handle appeals from the lower courts in six regions of California. Appeals concern broader issues than those of fact, which are settled at the lower court levels, and can involve proper trial procedure, correct interpretation of a law or a constitution (state or federal), or proper application of a law.

cross-filing When candidates attempt to gain the nomination of political parties to which they do not belong.

Department of Finance (DOF) The executive agency in charge of preparing the budget.

elite public The most knowledgeable segment of the population on a given issue.

executive budget A unified financial request of all agencies and departments, which is presented by the governor to the legislature as a single document.

federal funds Program grants received from the federal government.

general election An election in which the winner becomes the holder of the office in question.

general fund budget A component of the state budget in which most items normally associated with the state, such as education and welfare, are placed.

general law city A city that is governed according to specific provisions in the California Code.

incumbent An officeholder who seeks reelection.

independent state grounds doctrine A doctrine, advanced by various legal scholars and judges, that a state constitution can provide for rights that a person may not have in a U.S. federal court. In California, the doctrine has been applied in the case of criminal defendants, abortion, and the power of initiatives to control the power of the courts.

Johnson, Hiram A leading Progressive politician of California and national figure who was governor and then senator from 1911 to 1945. He promoted an array of Progressive measures, including the initiative and referendum, which would drive partisan politics out of the political process.

Judicial Performance Commission A commission that comprises judges and non-attorney citizens and that monitors judicial conduct.

LAFCO A local agency formation commission comprised of county government officials who make decisions on such issues as urban sprawl and secession.

Legislative Analyst's Office (LAO) The nonpartisan legislative agency that provides fiscal analysis.

line item veto The governor's ability to veto specific items in a budget bill without rejecting the entire piece of legislation.

mail ballot A ballot cast before election day and mailed to an appropriate county official.

mass public Those who do not have detailed knowledge of a particular political issue.

muckraking A style of journalism that is devoted to exposing corruption in business and government.

natural rights The inherent rights that all human beings are born with, regardless of time and geography. By limiting the power of government through the requirement that all legitimate power be based on consent, the natural rights doctrines of thinkers such as John Locke (1632–1704) provided the basis for American constitutional government and the first California Constitution.

new media Talk radio, cable television, and the Internet.

nonpartisan election An election for local offices, judicial positions, and the superintendent of public instruction.

operators, managers, and executives The three-tiered organizational scheme of a bureaucracy.

partisan election An election for legislative and statewide offices.

plural executive An executive branch headed by more than one elected official.

plurality The most votes in an election; could be less than a majority in a race of more than two candidates.

political question A deeply partisan political issue generally to be decided by the elected branches of government, not the courts, such as the question of who should be elected president.

president pro tempore The most powerful member of the forty-seat California Senate.

primary election An election that determines who will be the final contestants in the general election.

progressive tax A tax rate that increases as income rises.

Progressivism A broad-ranging reform movement intended to drive corrupt practices and party bosses out of politics and develop a powerful state led by enlightened administrators.

proportional representation (PR) A method of allocating seats in a legislature on the basis of the total percentage received in a national election.

redistricting Redrawing legislative districts to reflect population shifts.

regional association A quasi-governmental association of counties.

regressive tax A tax rate that decreases as income rises.

Rules Committee A key committee in each chamber that assigns bills to a particular committee, thus affecting their chances of passage.

sample A portion of a population used for polling.

self-interest rightly understood The understanding that it is in one's self-interest to guard the public liberty.

single member district (SMD) system A method of allocating seats in a legislature on the basis of a series of elections in specific districts.

speaker of the assembly The presiding officer in the eighty-seat assembly.

special district A unit of government created for a narrow purpose.

special funds Money earmarked for specific state programs.

stratified random distribution A method of constructing a sample that recreates the demographic conditions found in the population.

superior court Courts that try criminal and civil cases, including divorces.

supreme court The California Supreme Court consists of seven justices, who serve for twelve-year terms. It has original jurisdiction in a narrow range of cases, but its major impact is as an appellate court, reviewing the state courts of appeal decisions that are appealed to it.

term limits Restrictions on the total number of years a person may serve in a particular political office, such as the assembly, senate, or governorship.

third party Any party that is not one of the two major parties.

tyranny of the majority When the majority makes individuals unwilling to think a politically significant thought beyond the beliefs of their peers. The supposed deference of individuals to the majority's presumed wisdom is actually their willingness to flatter majority views in order to be accepted.

Warren, Earl A nationally renowned Progressive political leader who served as California's attorney general, then as governor for three terms. In 1954, he was appointed chief justice of the U.S. Supreme Court, a position he held until 1969.

yellow journalism A style of journalism devoted to supernatural stories, conspiracy theories, and gossip.

Notes

Preface to the Fourth Edition

1. Alexis de Tocqueville, *Democracy in America*, trans., ed., and with an introduction by Harvey C. Mansfield and Delba Winthrop (Chicago: University of Chicago Press, 2000), 7.

2. California Department of Finance, http://www.dof.ca.gov/HTML/FS_DATA/LatestEconData/documents/BBRANK.XLS (accessed January 20, 2015).

3. Basic information about California can be found at the following website: http://quickfacts.census.gov/qfd/states/06000.html (accessed January 20, 2015).

Introduction

1. Alexis de Tocqueville, *Democracy in America*, trans., ed., and with an introduction by Harvey C. Mansfield and Delba Winthrop (Chicago: University of Chicago Press, 2000), 13.

2. Harvey C. Mansfield and Delba Winthrop, introduction to Tocqueville, *Democracy in America*, xvii.

3. Tocqueville, *Democracy in America*. Among the better new editions are *Tocqueville: Democracy in America*, ed. and trans. Arthur Goldhammer (New York: Library of America, 2004); and a bilingual edition indispensable for scholars, Eduardo Nolla, ed., and James T. Schleifer, trans., *Democracy in America* (Indianapolis, IN: Liberty Fund, 2010).

4. See California Secretary of State, Voter Participation Statistics by County, http://elections.cdn.sos.ca.gov/sov/2014-general/pdf/03-voter-particpiation-stats-by-county.pdf (accessed January 19, 2015).

5. See Robert D. Putnam, *Bowling Alone: The Collapse and Revival of American Community* (New York: Simon & Schuster, 2000); and Francis Fukuyama, *The Great Disruption: Human Nature and the Reconstitution of Social Order* (New York: Touchstone Books, 1999).

6. Tocqueville, *Democracy in America*, 643.

7. Tocqueville, *Democracy in America*, 50.

8. Tocqueville, *Democracy in America*, 387–88.

9. Tocqueville, *Democracy in America*, 50.

10. Tocqueville, *Democracy in America*, vol. 2, part 2, chaps. 2–4.

11. For two contemporary works that emphasize the differences and continuity between Tocqueville's America and ours today, see Robert Bellah et al., *Habits of the Heart* (Berkeley: University of California, 1985); and Angelo Codevilla, *The Character of Nations: How Politics Makes and Breaks Prosperity, Family, and Civility* (New York: HarperCollins, Basic Books, 1997).

12. Robert J. Samuelson, "Who Cares How Rich Bill Gates Is?" *Washington Post*, May 2, 2001, A21.

13. Tocqueville, *Democracy in America*, 52.

14. Alexander Hamilton, James Madison, and John Jay, *The Federalist Papers*, ed. Clinton Rossiter with introduction and notes by Charles R. Kesler (New York: Penguin, Mentor Books, 1999), 346.

15. Several of these essays cited in *Democracy in California* previously appeared in *Nexus: A Journal of Opinion*, published by Chapman University Law School. These contributors are Herman Belz, Gordon Lloyd, Steven Hayward, Jack Pitney, Edward J. Erler, and Brian P. Janiskee. Readers will find these essays in *The California Republic*, plus work by, among others, Ward Connerly, Jon Coupal, Steven Frates, Victor Davis Hanson, Harold Johnson, Brian Kennedy, John Marini, Larry Peterman, Ralph Rossum, and Dan Walters.

Chapter 1. Diversity

1. Alexis de Tocqueville, *Democracy in America*, trans., ed., and with an introduction by Harvey C. Mansfield and Delba Winthrop (Chicago: University of Chicago Press, 2000), 392. Earlier, in footnote 19 (319), Tocqueville had warned of this problem: "Something more striking still is taking place in the province of Texas; the state of Texas, as we know, makes up a part of Mexico and serves as its frontier with the United States. For some years, the Anglo-Americans entered individually into this still ill-populated province, bought lands, took possession of industry, and rapidly substituted themselves for the original population. It can be foreseen that if Mexico does not hasten to halt this movement, it will not be long before Texas escapes from it."

2. Tocqueville, *Democracy in America*, 190.

3. Victor Davis Hanson, *The Land Was Everything* (New York: Free Press, 2000), 24–25.

4. Kevin Starr, *Material Dreams: Southern California through the 1920s* (New York: Oxford University Press, 1990), 69.

5. Richard Rodriguez, *Days of Obligation: Arguments with My Mexican Father* (New York: Viking, 1992), 28.

6. Starr, *Material Dreams*, 3.

7. For provocative thoughts on California demographics—population traits—see the work of Joel Kotkin. http://www.joelkotkin.com (accessed February 2, 2015). Constantly updated information on California can be found on California's website: http://www.ca.gov/index.asp (accessed February 2, 2015).

8. Rodriguez, *Days of Obligation*, 169.

9. Rodriguez, *Days of Obligation*, 63–64.

10. Legislative Analyst's Office, http://www.lao.ca.gov/ballot/2013/130771.aspx (accessed January 15, 2015).

11. Particularly damaging for students who might otherwise comprehend the greatness of the Founding Fathers is the disputable notion that they were racist, sexist, and classist. For a defense of the Founders against such criticism, see Thomas G. West, *Vindicating the Founders: Race, Sex, Class, and Justice in the Origins of America* (Lanham, MD: Rowman & Littlefield, 1997). See also Edward J. Erler, Thomas G. West, and John Marini, *The Founders on Citizenship and Immigration: Principles and Challenges in America* (Lanham, MD: Rowman & Littlefield, 2007).

12. James Madison, *The Federalist*, no. 10 (1787).

13. For an insightful study of George Washington's farewell address, see Matthew Spalding and Patrick Garrity, *A Sacred Union of Citizens: George Washington's Farewell Address and the American Character*, introduction by Daniel J. Boorstin (Lanham, MD: Rowman & Littlefield, 1996).

14. See Harry V. Jaffa, *Crisis of the House Divided: An Interpretation of the Issues in the Lincoln-Douglas Debates* (Chicago: University of Chicago Press, 1982, originally published by Oxford University Press, 1959); and Harry V. Jaffa, *A New Birth of Freedom: Abraham Lincoln and the Coming of the Civil War* (Lanham, MD: Rowman & Littlefield, 2000).

15. Aristotle, *The Politics of Aristotle*, ed. Peter L. Phillips Simpson (Chapel Hill: University of North Carolina Press, 1997), Book I. This is the best edition for students.

16. Abraham Lincoln, Address, "Address before the Wisconsin State Agricultural Society, Milwaukee, Wisconsin," September 30, 1859, in *Collected Works*, vol. 3 (New Brunswick, NJ: Rutgers University Press, 1953), 471–72.

17. Malcolm J. Rohrbough, *Days of Gold: The California Gold Rush and the American Nation* (Berkeley: University of California Press, 1997), 2. Alexander Hamilton's son, William Stephen Hamilton, died in August 1850 in Sacramento. Jefferson might have sneered at his pursuit of gold, but Alexander Hamilton might have approved, and those differences sum up the new America that arose through the enormous changes, or emphases, gold brought about. Tocqueville compares the westward movement of Americans with "what happened at the fall of the Roman Empire" (*Democracy in America*, 269). What might he have said about the Gold Rush! See also Kevin Starr, *Americans and the California Dream, 1850–1915* (New York: Oxford University Press, 1973), 54.

18. James Bryce, *The American Commonwealth*, vol. 2 (Indianapolis, IN: Liberty Fund Press, 1995), 1066.

19. The Gold Rush camps, though often enough scenes of violence, managed to produce an order based on commonsense property rights. According to journalist and activist Carey McWilliams, the miners sought to "safeguard the equality of opportunity which had prevailed at the outset." In addition to barring slavery, other measures were taken to ensure equality and to limit the size of each claim. See Carey McWilliams, *California: The Great Exception* (Berkeley: University of California, 1949; reprinted in 1999, with foreword by Lewis H. Lapham), 28. For analyses by economists, see Terry L. Anderson and P. J. Hill, "An American Experiment in Anarcho-Capitalism: The *Not* So Wild, Wild West," *Journal of Libertarian Studies* 3, no. 1 (Spring 1979): 9–28; and "The Evolution of Property Rights: A Study of the American West," *Journal of Law and Economics* 28, no. 1 (April 1975), 163–79.

20. Herman Belz, "Popular Sovereignty, The Right of Revolution, and California Statehood," in *The California Republic*, eds. Brian P. Janiskee and Ken Masugi (Lanham, MD: Rowman & Littlefield, 2004), 3–31.

21. California Constitution, Art. I, sec. 1 (1849). Currently this article, as revised on November 5, 1974, reads, "All people are by nature free and independent and have inalienable rights. Among these are enjoying and defending life and liberty, acquiring, possessing, and protecting property, and pursuing and obtaining safety, happiness, *and privacy*" (italics added).

22. The California Constitution has 54,645 words. The U.S. Constitution has 4,543 words. See Council of State Governments, http://knowledgecenter.csg.org/kc/content/book-states-2010-chapter-1-state-constitutions (accessed January 20, 2015); National Archives, http://www.archives.gov/exhibits/charters/constitution_q_and_a .html (accessed January 20, 2015).

23. Gordon Lloyd, "Nature and Convention in the Creation of the 1849 California Constitution," in *The California Republic*, 33–66.

24. James Madison, *The Federalist*, nos. 10 (1787) and 51 (1788).

25. Thomas Jefferson, Address, "First Inaugural Address," March 4, 1801, in Merrill Peterson, ed., *Jefferson* (New York: Library of America, 1984), 492–93.

26. Madison, *The Federalist*, no. 49 (1788).

27. For a positive view of the railroads and the men who made them, from the Big Four to the Chinese immigrants, see Stephen E. Ambrose, *Nothing Like It in the World: The Men Who Built the Transcontinental Railroad 1863–1869* (New York: Simon & Schuster, 2000), 17. Ambrose describes the transcontinental railroad—he does not discuss California's Central Pacific Railroad—as "the greatest achievement of the American people in the nineteenth century," surpassed only by the Civil War and the abolition of slavery.

28. California Constitution, Art. XIX, sec. 1, sec. 4 (1879).

29. Charles J. McClain, *In Search of Equality: The Chinese Struggle against Discrimination in Nineteenth-Century America* (Berkeley: University of California Press, 1994). More on the Chinese and other ethnic groups will appear in chapter 2.

30. McClain, *In Search of Equality*, 12.

31. Peter Skerry, *Mexican-Americans: The Ambivalent Minority* (New York: Free Press, 1993), 377–78. See also Samuel Huntington, "The Special Case of Mexican Immigration: Why Mexico Is a Problem," *American Enterprise* (December 2000), 22. Huntington writes, "Mexican immigration looms as a unique and disturbing

challenge to our cultural integrity, our national identity, and potentially to our future as a country." Robert Samuelson notes the difference between older waves of immigrants and recent Mexican immigrants: "Candor on Immigration," *Washington Post*, June 8, 2005, A21.

32. Peter Skerry, "Mexican Immigration Is Different," *American Enterprise* (December 2000), 22.

33. Skerry, *Mexican-Americans*, 9–10.

34. On recent controversies over immigration, see Carol M. Swain, ed., *Debating Immigration* (New York: Cambridge University Press, 2007). On race, see Stephan and Abigail Thernstrom, *America in Black and White: One Nation, Indivisible* (New York: Simon & Schuster, 1997).

35. See Diana L. Eck's fulsome account in *A New Religious America: How a "Christian Country" Has Become the World's Most Religiously Diverse Nation* (San Francisco: Harper San Francisco, 2001).

36. Rodriguez, *Days of Obligation*, 169.

37. Skerry, *Mexican-Americans*, 362–65.

38. Public Policy Institute of California, "California's Likely Voters," http://www.ppic.org/main/publication_show.asp?i=255 (accessed January 20, 2015). An older but comprehensive study by Jack Citrin and Benjamin Highton, *How Race, Ethnicity, and Immigration Shape the California Electorate* (San Francisco: Public Policy Institute of California, 2002), can be found on the publisher's website at http://www.ppic.org/content/pubs/report/R_1202JCR.pdf (accessed January 20, 2015).

Approximately one in four voters was from Los Angeles County; one in three were from the rest of Southern California.

39. Public Policy Institute of California, "California's Likely Voters."

40. Tocqueville, *Democracy in America*, 236.

41. Janet Zimmerman, "Groups Awaiting Arrival of Migrant Detainees in Murrieta," *Orange County Register*, http://www.ocregister.com/articles/murrieta-627978-detainees-protesters.html (accessed January 25, 2015); BBC News, "Protesters Block Migrant Busses in California," http://www.bbc.com/news/world-us-canada-28121198 (accessed January 25, 2015).

42. Max Ehrenfreund, "Your Complete Guide to Obama's Immigration Executive Action," *Washington Post*, http://www.washingtonpost.com/blogs/wonkblog/wp/2014/11/19/your-complete-guide-to-obamas-immigration-order/ (accessed January 22, 2015).

43. Scott Clement, "Do Americans Want to Stop Obama's Immigration Move? Yes and No." *Washington Post*, http://www.washingtonpost.com/blogs/the-fix/wp/2015/01/20/do-people-want-to-stop-obamas-immigration-move-yes-and-no/ (accessed January 25, 2015).

44. Victor Davis Hanson, *Mexifornia: A State of Becoming* (San Francisco: Encounter Books, 2007). In a subsequent piece, Hanson concludes that in accommodating illegal immigrants California has turned itself into a lawless, third-world state: "California is at once both the nation's most unfree and most free state, the most repressed and the wildest." "Two Californias," *National Review Online*, http://www.nationalreview.com/articles/255320/two-californias-victor-davis-hanson (accessed February 2, 2015).

Chapter 2. A Progressive Constitution

1. Alexis de Tocqueville, *Democracy in America*, trans., ed., and with an introduction by Harvey C. Mansfield and Delba Winthrop (Chicago: University of Chicago Press, 2000), 644–45.

2. George Washington Plunkitt, as recorded by William L. Riordon, *Plunkitt of Tammany Hall* (New York: Dutton, 1963), 39. The conversations of Boss Plunkitt with journalist Riordan were originally published in 1905 and contained chapters whose titles include "Honest Graft and Dishonest Graft," "Dangers of the Dress Suit in Politics," and "Bosses Preserve the Nation."

3. Primary texts for understanding Progressivism include Herbert Croly, *The Promise of American Life* (New York: Capricorn, 1964, originally published 1909); Charles Beard, *An Economic Interpretation of the Constitution of the United States* (New York: Macmillan, 1913); and the works of John Dewey, especially *The Public and Its Problems* (Chicago: Swallow, 1927). More generally, see John Marini and Ken Masugi, eds., *The Progressive Revolution in Politics and Political Science* (Lanham, MD: Rowman & Littlefield, 2005) and the increasingly influential work of Ronald J. Pestritto, *Woodrow Wilson and the Roots of Modern Liberalism* (Lanham, MD: Rowman & Littlefield, 2005). For an academic critique of Progressivism, see Thomas Silver, *Coolidge and the Historians* (Durham, NC: Carolina Academic Press, 1982).

4. See George E. Mowry, *The California Progressives* (Chicago: Quadrangle, 1963; originally published by University of California Press, 1951), 12. Perhaps too cynically, Mowry contended that for all the power of the railroad, the state "corrupted itself." If it weren't the railroad, he believed, it would have been something else.

5. Mowry, *California Progressives*, 87–91.

6. Frank Norris, *The Octopus: A Story of California* (New York: New American Library, Signet Classics, 1964; originally published 1901), 215. *The Octopus* is a novel based on contemporary California events, in which callous railroad owners destroy the lives of decent, hardworking ranchers, farmers, and immigrants.

7. G. Alan Tarr, *Understanding State Constitutions* (Princeton, NJ: Princeton University Press, 2000), 148.

8. Mowry, *California Progressives*, 113–16. Mowry does not paint an appealing portrait: This reformer appears to fulfill virtually every cliché about a hack politician. Not an intellectual or a cultured man, he was "a sensitive and thin-skinned rebel . . . nervous, moody, and insecure."

9. For Johnson's achievements, see Mowry, *California Progressives*; and Olin, *Prodigal Sons*. These terms are discussed in this and later chapters.

10. John Aubrey Douglass, *The California Idea and American Higher Education* (Stanford, CA: Stanford University Press, 2000), 82.

11. Earl Warren, *The Memoirs of Chief Justice Earl Warren* (Garden City, NY: Doubleday, 1977), 171. Kevin Starr describes "Honey Bear" Warren's glowing political talents; see *Embattled Dreams: California in War and Peace, 1940–1950* (New York: Oxford University Press, 2002), 241–80.

12. *California: An Illustrated History* (New York: Van Nostrand, 1968), 97.

13. See, among others, Kevin Starr, *Endangered Dreams: The Great Depression in California* (New York: Oxford University Press, 1996). For a general history of California that emphasizes leftist radicals' influence on the development of politics and culture, see Stephen Schwartz, *From West to East: California and the Making of the American Mind* (New York: Free Press, 1998). On the evolution of Progressivism, see the work of Sidney M. Milkis, particularly *Theodore Roosevelt, the Progressive Party, and the Transformation of American Democracy* (Lawrence: University Press of Kansas, 2009).

14. Steven Hayward, "Ronald Reagan and the Transformation of Modern California," in *The California Republic*, ed. Brian P. Janiskee and Ken Masugi (Lanham, MD: Rowman & Littlefield, 2004), 237–53; John J. Pitney, "Nixon, California, and American Politics," in *The California Republic*, 219–35; and Steven Hayward, *The Age of Reagan, 1964–1980: The Fall of the Old Liberal Order* (New York: Prima, 2001) and *The Age of Reagan: The Conservative Counterrevolution: 1980–1989.* (New York: Crown Forum, 2009).

15. Article IX, section 1, on education, reads, "A general diffusion of knowledge and intelligence being essential to the preservation of the rights and liberties of the people, the Legislature shall encourage by all suitable means the promotion of intellectual, scientific, moral, and agricultural improvement." Compare this with the Northwest Ordinance's preconstitutional declaration: "Religion, morality, and knowledge, being necessary to good government and the happiness of mankind, schools and the means of education shall forever be encouraged." Northwest Ordinance, article 3, in *Documents of American History*, ed. Henry Steele Commager (Englewood Cliffs, NJ: Prentice Hall, 1973), vol. 1, 131.

16. E. Dotson Wilson and Brian S. Ebbert, *California's Legislature* (Sacramento: California State Legislature, Office of the Chief Clerk of the Assembly, 1998), 16.

17. The relationship between the two constitutions has become more complicated in recent years. In 1965, the California Supreme Court invented a new doctrine of "independent state grounds," an attempt to confine questions that are covered in federal case law to state courts when the state constitution has language similar to that of the U.S. Constitution. Thus, a Californian could have more rights as a state citizen (e.g., as a criminal defendant) than he or she might have in the federal courts as a U.S. citizen. For more on this theme, see chapter 8, "The Courts."

18. California Constitution Revision Commission, "Opposing Views," in *Final Report and Recommendations to the Governor and the Legislature* (Sacramento: State of California, 1996), 85–98.

19. See Bruce E. Cain and Roger G. Noll, eds., *Constitutional Reform in California* (Berkeley, CA: Institute of Governmental Studies Press, 1995).

20. Mowry, *California Progressives*, 301.

21. Edward J. Erler, "Californians and Their Constitution: Progressivism, Direct Democracy, and the Administrative State," in *The California Republic*, 118–19.

22. Peter Schrag, *Paradise Lost: California's Experience, America's Future* (Berkeley: University of California Press, 1998), 271. See as well William Voegeli, "Failed State," *Claremont Review of Books*, http://www.claremont.org/article/failed-state1/#.VM_t8mjF_To (accessed February 2, 2015).

23. California Secretary of State, "Proposition 209: Text of Proposed Law," http://vote96.sos.ca.gov/html/BP/209text.htm (accessed January 25, 2015).

24. For a balanced insider account of this struggle, see Lydia Chavez, *The Color Bind: California's Battle to End Affirmative Action* (Berkeley: University of California Press, 1998). Chairman Ward Connerly of the Proposition 209 campaign subsequently wrote a moving autobiography, *Creating Equal: My Fight against Race Preferences* (San Francisco: Encounter Books, 2000). He subsequently carried his fight successfully to Washington State (Initiative 200, 1998) and Michigan (Proposal 2, 2006).

25. Katy Murphy, "California's Affirmative Action Ban Bolstered by Supreme Court Ruling," *San Jose Mercury News*, http://www.mercurynews.com/education/ci_25617295/californias-affirmative-action-ban-bolstered-by-supreme-court (accessed January 25, 2015).

26. Center for Investigative Reporting, http://californiawatch.org/dailyreport/despite-diversity-efforts-uc-minority-enrollment-down-prop-209-15031 (accessed January 25, 2015).

27. *San Jose Mercury News*, "California's Affirmative Action Ban Bolstered by Supreme Court Ruling,"

Chapter 3. Public Opinion and the Media

1. Alexis de Tocqueville, *Democracy in America*, trans., ed., and with an introduction by Harvey C. Mansfield and Delba Winthrop (Chicago: University of Chicago Press, 2000), 243.

2. Tocqueville, *Democracy in America*, 177.

3. Joseph M. Bessette, *The Mild Voice of Reason* (Chicago: University of Chicago Press, 1994), 35.

4. For an outstanding account of face-to-face interaction between political leaders and their constituents, see Richard F. Fenno Jr., *Homestyle* (Boston: Little, Brown, 1978).

5. John W. Kingdon, *Congressmen's Voting Decisions*, 3rd ed. (Ann Arbor: University of Michigan Press, 1989).

6. Anthony Downs, "Up and Down with Ecology: The 'Issue Attention Cycle,'" *The Public Interest* 28 (Summer 1972): 38–50.

7. Sharon Bernstein and Robert A. Rosenblatt, "Average HMO Medicare Rate Set to Double," *Los Angeles Times*, September 16, 2000, 1.

8. Susan Warner, "Drug Firms Get a Dose of Disdain in This Election Year," *San Diego Union-Tribune*, September 2, 2000, C1.

9. *The Federalist*, 288–93.

10. Today, ideology is synonymous with political prejudice, and its connotation is that all political opinions are equally groundless. Since, in the modern mind, there are no natural standards, the expression of opinion is merely the expression of will. While we are forced to use the term *ideology* because of its ubiquitous quality, we mean something more like political opinion as opposed to political will. For a reasonably ac-

cessible discussion of this, see Leo Strauss and Joseph Cropsey, "Introduction," in *History of Political Philosophy*, 3rd ed. (Chicago: University of Chicago Press, 1987), 1–6.

11. It is a matter of debate just what it is that conservatives defend. A misunderstanding of the nature of the thing to be defended could have profound and lasting effects. See Harry V. Jaffa, *American Conservatism and the American Founding* (Durham, NC: Carolina Academic Press, 1984).

12. Louise G. White, *Political Analysis* (Pacific Grove, CA: Brooks/Cole, 1990).

13. Josh Getlin, "Regarding the Media: For Whom the Polls Toll—The Candidate Who's Trailing," *Los Angeles Times*, September 18, 2000, E1. See also Bruce Bimber, Jennifer Brundidge, Meredith Conroy, and Erica Lively. "Issue Comparisons and Ordinal Priming," *International Journal of Communication* (7): 1053–73.

14. Michael Taylor, "The Reign of S.F.'s Monarch of the Dailies; Hearst Media Empire Started with Examiner," *San Francisco Chronicle*, August 2, 1999, A9.

15. Jeff Gottlieb and Ruben Vives, "Is a City Manager Worth $800,000?," *Los Angeles Times*, http://www.latimes.com/news/local/la-me-bell-salary-20100715,0,7352605. story (accessed February 2, 2015); David Folkenflik, "How the L.A. Times Broke the Bell Corruption Story," *NPR*, http://www.npr.org/templates/story/story .php?storyId=130108851 (accessed February 2, 2015).

16. Wyatt Buchanan, "How Much Does Your City Pay Its Manager? Look Here." *San Francisco Chronicle*, http://www.sfgate.com/cgi-bin/blogs/nov05election/ detail?entry_id=72074 (accessed February 2, 2015).

17. Michael Martinez, "Voters Recall Councilmen in Scandal-plagued California City," *CNN*, http://www.cnn.com/2011/CRIME/03/10/california.bell.scandal/ (accessed January 29, 2015).

18. J. Patrick Coolican, "City of Bell Officials Arrested," *LA Weekly*, http://blogs. laweekly.com/informer/2010/09/city_of_bell_officials_arreste.php# (accessed February 2, 2015).

19. Corina Knoll and Jeff Gottlieb, "Rizzo Gets 12 Years in Prison, Marking End to Scandal That Rocked Bell," *Los Angeles Times*, http://www.latimes.com/local/ lanow/la-me-ln-rizzo-set-to-be-sentenced--20140415-story.html (accessed January 29, 2015).

20. Corina Knoll and Kate Mather, "Former Bell Official Angela Spaccia Gets 11 years, 8 Months in Prison," *Los Angeles Times*, http://articles.latimes.com/2014/ apr/10/local/la-me-ln-angela-spaccia-bell-prison-20140410 (accessed January 29, 2015).

21. Corina Knoll, "Former Bell Councilwoman Teresa Jacobo Gets Two-Year Prison Sentence," *Los Angeles Times*, http://www.latimes.com/local/la-me-bell-sen tence-20140726-story.html (accessed January 29, 2015).

22. Ruben Vives, "Ex-Bell Mayor's Store Is Vandalized with Graffiti after Sentencing," *Los Angeles Times*, http://www.latimes.com/local/lanow/la-me-ln-ex-bell -mayor-store-graffiti-20140801-story.html (accessed January 29, 2015); *CBS News, Los Angeles*, "Former Bell City Councilman Sentenced To Probation, 1 Year in Jail," http://losangeles.cbslocal.com/2014/07/11/former-bell-city-councilman-sentenced- to-probation-1-year-in-jail/ (accessed January 29, 2015); Corina Knoll, "Final Bell

Council Member Sentenced," *Los Angeles Times* http://www.latimes.com/local/poli tics/la-me-0802-bell-finale-20140802-story.html (accessed January 29, 2015).

23. Jeff Gottlieb, "Former Bell Mayor George Cole Gets Home Confinement in Corruption Case," *Los Angeles Times*, http://www.latimes.com/local/lanow/la-me -ln-former-bell-mayor-sentenced-20140723-story.html (accessed January 29, 2015).

24. *Los Angeles Daily News*, "Former Bell Police Chief to Reimburse City for over $200,000 in Tentative Settlement," http://www.dailynews.com/general -news/20140410/former-bell-police-chief-to-reimburse-city-for-over-200000-in-ten tative-settlement (accessed January 29, 2015).

25. The Pulitzer Prizes, http://www.pulitzer.org/bycat/Public-Service (accessed January 29, 2015).

Chapter 4. Parties and Interest Groups

1. Alexis de Tocqueville, *Democracy in America*, trans., ed., and with an introduc- tion by Harvey C. Mansfield and Delba Winthrop (Chicago: University of Chicago Press, 2000), 185.

2. See Harry V. Jaffa, "The Nature and Origin of the American Party System," in *Equality and Liberty* (New York: Oxford University Press, 1965), 3–41. However, this is true only so long as the principles of the American Revolution are the animating principles of the regime.

3. Kathleen Les, "Business's Big Guns," in *California Government and Politics An- nual 1998–1999* (Sacramento, CA: StateNet, 1999), 43–44; Kathleen Les, "Labor Toils Mightily for a Select Few," *California Journal* 31 (May 2000): 46–49; and Cynthia H. Craft, "The Economic Silver Lining to Gun Laws," *California Journal* 31 (March 2000): 18–22.

4. The rise in strength of interest groups has coincided with the decline of parties. See evidence of this in Norman Ornstein, Thomas Mann, and Michael Malbin, *Vital Statistics on Congress, 1993–1994* (Washington, D.C.: U.S. Government Printing Of- fice, 1994). Further confirmation of this trend can be found in L. Harmon Zigler and Hendrik van Dalen, "Interest Groups in the States," in *Politics in the American States*, 2nd ed., eds. Herbert Jacob and Kenneth N. Vines (Boston: Little, Brown, 1974), 122–60.

5. Elections for local offices, judicial positions, and the superintendent of public instruction are nonpartisan.

6. When a citizen registers to vote in California, he or she is given the option of declaring a political party preference. Voters register for a political party when they identify themselves with such a party on their voter registration form. For more information of political party qualifications, see the California Secretary of State's de- scription of these requirements at https://www.sos.ca.gov/elections/political-parties/ political-party-qualification.htm (accessed January 29, 2015).

7. California Secertary of State, 2014 Election Results by County, http://elections. cdn.sos.ca.gov/sov/2014-general/pdf/03-voter-particpiation-stats-by-county.pdf (ac- cessed January 15, 2015).

8. California Secretary of State, "Qualified Political Parties," https://www.sos
.ca.gov/elections/political-parties/qualified-political-party.htm (accessed January 29,
2015).

9. Robert DiClerico, *Political Parties, Campaigns and Elections* (Upper Saddle
River, NJ: Prentice Hall, 2000).

10. In addition to this account, one might consider the effects of divided government in California. Because of the initiative/referendum/recall process, it is likely
that the effects of divided government are even less pronounced in California. For
a further discussion, see David Mayhew, *Divided We Govern* (New Haven, CT: Yale
University Press, 1991); Morris Fiorina, *Divided Government*, 2nd ed. (New York:
Allyn and Bacon, 1996); and Peter F. Galderisi, ed., *Divided Government: Change, Uncertainty, and the Constitutional Order* (Lanham, MD: Rowman & Littlefield, 1996).

11. *The Federalist*, 45–52.

12. E. E. Schattschneider, *The Semi-Sovereign People* (New York: Holt, Rinehart,
& Winston, 1960).

13. David B. Truman, *The Governmental Process: Political Interests and Public
Opinion* (New York: Knopf, 1951).

14. Mancur Olson Jr., *The Logic of Collective Action* (New York: Schocken Books,
1968); and Jack Walker, *Mobilizing Interest Groups in America* (Ann Arbor: University of Michigan Press, 1991).

15. The Political Reform Division has the following official responsibilities: regulate state and local campaign committees that raise funds for nonfederal elections,
receive and verify campaign disclosure statements, regulate campaign documents,
provide public access to all campaign information, and impose fines and penal-
ties for failure to comply with regulations. For more information see the Political
Reform Division's website, http://www.sos.ca.gov/campaign-lobbying (accessed
January 29, 2015).

16. Conservative and business groups have been more effective in grassroots activity as of late. See Bill Ainsworth, "Astroturf Lobbying," *California Government and
Politics Annual: 1998–1999* (Sacramento, CA: StateNet, 1998), 39–40.

17. Carol S. Weissert and William S. Weissert, *Governing Health: The Politics of
Health Policy* (Baltimore, MD: Johns Hopkins University Press, 1996).

18. *Big Money Talks: California's Billion Dollar Club*, California Fair Political
Practices Commission, http://www.fppc.ca.gov/reports/Report31110.pdf (accessed
January 29, 2015), 10.

19. Gerald Mayer, "Union Membership Trends in the United States," Cornell University ILR School, http://digitalcommons.ilr.cornell.edu/cgi/viewcontent
.cgi?article=1176&context=key_workplace (accessed January 31, 2015), 12.

20. Barry Hirsch and David Macpherson, http://www.unionstats.com/ (accessed
January 31, 2015). The year 2009 was the first year in which there were more public
sector union members than those in the private sector.

21. Niraj Chokshi, "These 5 Maps Show Unions Are Losing Ground in the
States," *The Washington Post*, http://www.washingtonpost.com/blogs/govbeat/
wp/2014/01/27/these-5-maps-show-unions-are-losing-ground-in-the-states/ (accessed January 31, 2015).

Chapter 5. Campaigns and Elections

1. Alexis de Tocqueville, *Democracy in America*, trans., ed., and with an introduction by Harvey C. Mansfield and Delba Winthrop (Chicago: University of Chicago Press, 2000), 197.

2. John Dinan, "Framing a People's Government: State Constitution-Making in the Progressive Era," *Rutgers Law Journal* 30 (1999): 933–85.

3. Alan Rosenthal, *The Decline of Representative Democracy* (Washington, D.C.: Congressional Quarterly Press, 1997).

4. Brian P. Janiskee, "The United States Presidential Election of 2000: The Prospects for Controversy," *Talking Politics: The Journal of the Politics Association* 12 (Winter 2000): 337–42.

5. One should also include the District of Columbia, which acts as a state for purposes of electing a president. This is the result of the Twenty-third Amendment to the United States Constitution.

6. California Secretary of State, https://www.sos.ca.gov/elections/statewide-elections/2014-primary/qualifications.htm (accessed February 1, 2015).

7. *California Democratic Party v. Jones* (2000).

8. "Proposition 14," *Legislative Analyst's Office*, http://www.lao.ca.gov/ballot/2010/14_06_2010.aspx (accessed February 2, 2015).

9. "Initiative, Referendum, and Recall," *National Conference of State Legislatures*, http://www.ncsl.org/research/elections-and-campaigns/initiative-referendum-and-recall-overview.aspx (accessed February 2, 2015).

10. California Government Code, section 11221.

11. "Propositions," *California Journal* 31 (February 2000): 59–71.

12. Stephen M. Nichols, "State Referendum Voting, Ballot Roll-Off, and the Effect of New Electoral Technology," *State and Local Government Review* 30 (Spring 1998): 106–13.

13. Bessette, *Mild Voice of Reason.*

14. Michael Finnegan, "Neel Kashkari Spent More Than Jerry Brown on Governor's Race," *Los Angeles Times*, http://www.latimes.com/local/political/la-me-pc-kashkari-brown-campaign-spending-20150130-story.html (accessed February 1, 2015).

15. Steve Lopez, "Meg Whitman Spent $50 for Each Vote She Got. Is That an Outrageous Extravagance?," *Los Angeles Times*, http://latimesblogs.latimes.com/lanow/2010/11/steve-lopez-meg-whitman-spent-50-for-each-vote-she-got-is-that-an-outrageous-extravagance.html (accessed February 2, 2015).

16. Using the latest available Consumer Price Index (CPI) numbers, where 1982–1984 is 100, the gubernatorial election in 2010 was 9.28 times more expensive than the 1976 election in *real* terms. The CPI index for 1976 is 56.9 and for 2009, is 214.5. U.S. Department of Labor, Bureau of Labor Statistics, found in Seattle Government website, http://www.seattle.gov/financedepartment/cpi/documents/US_CPI_History_--_Annual_000.pdf (accessed February 2, 2015).

17. See *Buckley v. Valeo* (1976), *Nixon v. Shrink Missouri Government PAC* (2000), *Citizens United v. FEC* (2010).

18. John M. Carey, Richard G. Niemi, and Lynda W. Powell, "Incumbency and the Probability of Reelection in State Legislative Elections," *Journal of Politics* 62 (August 2000): 671–700.

19. Peverill Squire, "Uncontested Seats in State Legislative Elections," *Legislative Studies Quarterly* 25 (February 2000): 131–46.

20. Christopher Cadelago, "California's record-low voter turnout stirs anxieties," *Sacramento Bee*, http://www.sacbee.com/news/politics-government/election/article4237488.html (accessed February 1, 2015).

21. Robert D. Putnam, *Bowling Alone: The Collapse and Revival of American Community* (New York: Simon & Schuster, 2000).

22. Complete recall results can be found on the website for the California Secretary of State: http://elections.cdn.sos.ca.gov/sov/2003-special/sov-complete.pdf (accessed February 1, 2015).

Chapter 6. The Legislature

1. Alexis de Tocqueville, *Democracy in America*, trans., ed., and with an introduction by Harvey C. Mansfield and Delba Winthrop (Chicago: University of Chicago Press, 2000), 202.

2. James D. King, "Changes in Professionalism in U.S. State Legislatures," *Legislative Studies Quarterly* 25, no. 2 (2000): 327–43.

3. Peverill Squire, "Legislative Professionalism and Membership Diversity in State Legislatures," *Legislative Studies Quarterly* 17, no. 1 (1992): 69–79.

4. National Conference of State Legislatures, http://www.ncsl.org/research/about-state-legislatures/full-and-part-time-legislatures.aspx (accessed February 1, 2015).

5. National Conference of State Legislatures, http://www.ncsl.org/research/about-state-legislatures/2014-ncsl-legislator-salary-and-per-diem-table.aspx; http://www.ncsl.org/research/about-state-legislatures/legislative-session-length.aspx (accessed February 1, 2015).

6. Aristotle, *The Politics*, trans. and introduction by Carnes Lord (Chicago: University of Chicago Press, 1984), 114.

7. Joseph M. Bessette, *The Mild Voice of Reason* (Chicago: University of Chicago Press, 1994), 35.

8. For a convincing account of the Founders' belief that voters were capable of such a task, see Thomas G. West, *Vindicating the Founders: Race, Sex, Class, and Justice in the Origins of America* (Lanham, MD: Rowman & Littlefield, 1997), 111–30.

9. Edward J. Erler, *The American Polity* (Washington, D.C.: Crane Russak, 1991), 20–36, 59–67.

10. Nebraska has a unicameral legislature.

11. Tocqueville, *Democracy in America*, 81.

12. Martin Diamond, *The Founding of the Democratic Republic* (Itasca, IL: Peacock, 1981), 97; and William P. Bottom et al., "The Institutional Effect on Majority

Rule Instability: Bicameralism in Spatial Policy Decisions," *American Journal of Political Science* 44, no. 3 (2000): 523–40. See also Thomas H. Hammond and Gary J. Miller, "The Core of the Constitution," *American Political Science Review* 81 (1987): 1155–74.

13. *The Federalist Papers*, 250.

14. However, in extreme situations, one might be willing to accept extraordinary measures to save a republic.

15. Mark Rush, ed., *Voting Rights and Redistricting in the United States* (Westport, CT: Greenwood, 1999).

16. Bernard Grofman, ed., *Race and Redistricting in the 1990s* (New York: Agathon, 1999).

17. One might ask how the Supreme Court could come to this decision in light of the method of representation in the U.S. Senate. The answer is that the court recognized the sovereign nature of the states that formed the nation. Geographic subunits of states, such as counties, were never sovereign entities.

18. *Gerrymandering* is derived from the attempt of Massachusetts governor Elbridge Gerry to rig the 1812 election in favor of his party's legislative candidates. The key to successful gerrymandering is to split up the opposing party's base of support into portions of other districts in which the favored party has majorities.

19. Citizens Redistricting Commission, http://wedrawthelines.ca.gov/commission .html (accessed February 1, 2015).

20. Term limits have side effects: they force candidates to move "up or out," and many term-limited legislators try to move into Congress. See Michael Berkman and James Eisenstein, "State Legislators as Congressional Candidates," *Political Research Quarterly* 52, no. 3 (1999): 481–98; and John R. Hibbing, "Legislative Careers: Why and How We Should Study Them," *Legislative Studies Quarterly* 24, no. 2 (1999): 149–71. For some of the unanswered promises of term limits, see Dan Walters, "Legislature Risks Return to Elitism," *Fresno Bee*, 27 June 2000, A9.

21. National Conference of State Legislatures, http://www.ncsl.org/research/ about-state-legislatures/chart-of-term-limits-states.aspx (accessed February 1, 2015).

22. For examples of how the leadership helps organize each chamber at the beginning of a session see Patrick McGreevy, "Senate Leader Reshuffles Committee Chairs," *Los Angeles Times*, http://latimesblogs.latimes.com/california-politics/2011/01/sen ate-leader-reshuffles-committee-chairs.html (accessed February 2, 2015); Torey Van Oot, "Pérez Announces Leadership and Committee Assignments," *Sacramento Bee*, http://blogs.sacbee.com/capitolalertlatest/2010/12/perez-announces-dem-leadership .html (accessed February 2, 2015).

23. For a firsthand account of the process in California, see Michael J. BeVier, *Politics Backstage* (Philadelphia: Temple University Press, 1979).

24. Note that the assembly committees and senate committees may have different names and jurisdictional boundaries between committees. Each chamber is free to divide committee responsibilities as it sees fit. Committees change jurisdictions from time to time. New committees are created and old ones disbanded.

25. There are three types of committees: standing, select, and joint. Standing committees have regular jurisdictions and remain as entities until the chamber decides to

disband them. Select committees are temporary and charged with examining specific, narrowly focused issues. Once the issue is evaluated, the committee is dissolved. A joint committee contains members of both chambers and deals with specific items that affect both chambers simultaneously.

26. This is different from the U.S. Congress. In that chamber, only a majority *of those voting* is required, as long as a quorum exists.

27. Veto overrides are rare. In effect, a governor's veto nearly always defeats an act. However, if a governor suspects that the legislature would override a veto, the governor might allow an act to become law without a signature. This allows the governor to register disapproval without risking the embarrassment that would come with a legislative override of a veto.

28. Ben Adler, "It's Gut-and-Amend Time at the Capitol," Capital Public Radio, http://www.capradio.org/articles/2014/08/27/its-gut-and-amend-time-at-the-capitol/ (accessed February 1, 2015); Thomas D. Elias, "Will Arnold Try to End Gut-Amend?" *Daily News of Los Angeles*, August 30, 2004, N13; Greg Lucas and Matthew Yi, "At Session-End, Old Bills Take on Brand New Lives," *San Francisco Chronicle*, August 31, 2006, B2; Dan Walters, "Governor a Reformer? Actions on Two Bills Belie Rhetoric," *Sacramento Bee*, October 6, 2004, A3; Thomas D. Elias, "Gut and Amend?" *San Diego Union-Tribune*, August 18, 2004, B8.

29. Lucas and Yi, "Old Bills," B2.

30. "Gut and Amend?" *San Diego Union Tribune*, B8.

31. "Gut and Amend?" *San Diego Union Tribune*, B8.

Chapter 7. The Executive

1. Alexis de Tocqueville, *Democracy in America*, trans., ed., and with an introduction by Harvey C. Mansfield and Delba Winthrop (Chicago: University of Chicago Press, 2000), 81.

2. Charles Barrilleaux, "Governors, Bureaus, and State Policymaking," *State and Local Government Review* 21, no. 1 (1989): 53–59.

3. "Summary of Qualifications and Requirements for Independent Nomination for the Offices of Governor and Lieutenant Governor," California Secretary of State, https://www.sos.ca.gov/elections/statewide-elections/2014-primary/governor -lieutenant-governor-2014.htm (accessed February 2, 2015).

4. Sarah McCally Morehouse, *The Governor as Party Leader* (Ann Arbor: University of Michigan Press, 1998).

5. *Economist*, "Suddenly Brown's a Winner," May 22, 1976, 33.

6. Peter Goldman et al., "How Tight Can It Get?" *Newsweek*, July 12, 1976, 16.

7. Steve Scott, "Davis, the Political Powerhouse," *California Journal* 31 (August 2000): 28–31.

8. California Lieutenant Governor, http://www.ltg.ca.gov/m_about.html (accessed February 1, 2015).

9. Deanna Bellandi, "California Appeals Sutter-Summit Merger Ruling," *Modern Healthcare* 31 (January 2000): 4.

10. Julie Tamaki, "Teacher Pension System Dumps Tobacco Stock," *Los Angeles Times*, June 8, 2000, A3.

11. Jean O. Pasco, "Controller Sitting on a Pile of Money," *Los Angeles Times*, July 18, 2000, B2.

12. This is not to say that officeholders immediately lose their policy preferences on gaining office. The idea of a nonpartisan office is a residue of the Progressive movement's aim to install public officials who have "neutral competency." The most prevalent manifestation of this idea is with the creation and maintenance of a civil service.

13. Meredith May, "Little Improvement in Dropout Rates from California Schools," *San Francisco Chronicle*, June 9, 2000, A3.

14. James Q. Wilson, *Bureaucracy: What Government Agencies Do and Why They Do It* (New York: Basic Books, 1989).

15. Max Weber, "Bureaucracy," in *Max Weber: Essays in Sociology*, ed. H. H. Gerth and C. Wright Mills (New York: Oxford University Press, 1946), 196–244.

16. "Salaries of Elected Officials," *California Citizens Compensation Commission*, http://www.dpa.ca.gov/cccc/salaries/main.htm (accessed January 18, 2015); Larry Gordon, "UC leases housing at $9,950 a month for president Napolitano," *Los Angeles Times*, http://articles.latimes.com/2013/sep/16/local/la-me-ln-uc-rental-20130916 (accessed January 18, 2015).

17. Richard Coke Lower, *A Bloc of One: The Political Career of Hiram W. Johnson* (Stanford, CA: Stanford University Press, 1993); and Spencer Olin Jr., *California's Prodigal Sons: Hiram Johnson and the Progressives* (Berkeley: University of California Press, 1968).

18. Patricia Wallace Ingraham, *The Foundation of Merit: Public Service in American Democracy* (Baltimore, MD: Johns Hopkins University Press, 1995).

19. Arnold Schwarzenegger, State of the State Address, January 6, 2004, C-SPAN http://www.c-span.org/video/?179801-1/california-state-state-address (accessed February 2, 2015).

20. Mark Martin, Carla Marinucci, and Lynda Gledhill, "The Special Election; Californians Say No to Schwarzenegger," *San Francisco Chronicle*, November 9, 2005, A1.

Chapter 8. The Courts

1. Alexis de Tocqueville, *Democracy in America*, trans., ed., and with an introduction by Harvey C. Mansfield and Delba Winathrop (Chicago: University of Chicago Press, 2000), 94–95.

2. *The Federalist*, 465.

3. Alan W. Alschuler, *Law without Values: The Life, Work, and Legacy of Justice Holmes* (Chicago: University of Chicago Press, 2000).

4. *The Federalist*, 470–71.

5. Tocqueville, *Democracy in America*, 95.

6. Tocqueville, *Democracy in America*, 256.

7. *Raven v. Deukmejian* (1990). See later in this chapter for further discussion.

8. Joseph R. Grodin, *In Pursuit of Justice: Reflections of a State Supreme Court Justice*, with a foreword by Justice William J. Brennan Jr. (Berkeley: University of California Press, 1989), 230.

9. The Supreme Court website offers a summary of its development. See http://www.courts.ca.gov/documents/2007_Supreme_Court_Booklet_withInserts.pdf (accessed February 2, 2015).

10. John C. Eastman and Timothy Sandefur, "Stephen Field: Frontier Justice or Justice on the Natural Rights Frontier?" *Nexus: A Journal of Opinion* 6 (Spring 2001): 121–32. Field wrote the dissenting opinion in *The Slaughterhouse Cases* 83 U.S. 16 (1873). For Field and his contemporary judges, see also Charles J. McClain, *In Search of Equality: The Chinese Struggle against Discrimination in Nineteenth-Century America* (Berkeley: University of California Press, 1994).

11. Article VI, section 7.

12. California Courts Fact Sheet, http://www.courts.ca.gov/documents/Calif_Judicial_Branch.pdf (accessed January 19, 2015).

13. Richard K. De Atley, "How to Become a Judge?" *The Press-Enterprise* (Riverside), July 31, 2006, B1; California Courts, "Introduction," Court Statistics Report 2012–2013, http://www.courts.ca.gov/documents/2014-Court-Statistics-Report-Introduction.pdf (accessed January 18, 2015).

14. California Courts, http://www.courts.ca.gov/2948.htm (accessed January 18, 2015).

15. See Court Statistics Report 2012–2013.

16. Lincoln, June 26, 1857, in Roy P. Basler, ed., *The Collected Works of Abraham Lincoln*, vol. 2 (New Brunswick, NJ: Rutgers University Press, 1953), 400–401.

17. Howard Ball, *The Bakke Case: Race, Education, and Affirmative Action* (Lawrence: University Press of Kansas, 2000), 58. We have drawn liberally from Ball's account of the case.

18. For an evenhanded account of this contentious issue by a supporter of affirmative action, see Lydia Chavez, *The Color Bind: California's Battle to End Affirmative Action* (Berkeley: University of California Press, 1998).

19. *In re Marriage Cases* (2008).

20. Jessica Garrison and Joanna Lin, "Prop. 8 Protesters Target Mormon Temple in Westwood," *Los Angeles Times*, http://www.latimes.com/news/local/la-me-protest7-2008nov07,0,3827549.story (accessed February 2, 2015); Jim Carlton, "Gay Activists Boycott Backers of Prop. 8," *Wall Street Journal*, http://online.wsj.com/article/SB123033766467736451.html (accessed February 2, 2015).

21. *Hollingsworth v. Perry* (2013).

22. Brian P. Janiskee and Edward J. Erler, "Crime, Punishment and *Romero*: An Analysis of the Case against California's Three Strikes Law," *Duquesne Law Review* 39 (Fall 2000): 43–65 (cited by the court in *Ewing v. California*, 123 S.Ct.1179, 2003). The authors also take up the separation of powers issue that may arise if a judge is not given the discretion to impose a sentence of his own fashioning.

23. See Janiskee and Erler, "Crime, Punishment and *Romero*."

Chapter 9. The Budget and Government Finance

1. Alexis de Tocqueville, *Democracy in America*, trans., ed., and with an introduction by Harvey C. Mansfield and Delba Winthrop (Chicago: University of Chicago Press, 2000), 215.

2. See John Marini, *The Politics of Budget Control* (Washington, D.C.: Crane Russak, 1991).

3. California Constitution, article 4, section 12.

4. California Department of Finance, www.dof.ca.gov/fisa/bag/process.htm (accessed February 1, 2015).

5. Legislative Analyst's Office, *CAL Facts* (Sacramento, CA: Legislative Analyst's Office, 2000).

6. California Government Code, section 13337.5, and California Constitution, article 4, section 12.

7. Legislative Analysis' Office, "The 2013–14 Budget: California Spending Plan," http://lao.ca.gov/reports/2013/bud/spending-plan/spending-plan-073013.aspx (accessed January 18, 2015).

8. Governor's Budget 2013–2014, "Enacted Budget Detail," http://www.ebudget .ca.gov/2013-14/Enacted/agencies.html (accessed January 18, 2015).

9. Governor's Budget 2013–2014, "Enacted Budget Summary," http://www.ebud get.ca.gov/2013-14/pdf/Enacted/BudgetSummary/SummaryCharts.pdf (accessed January 18, 2015).

10. The logic behind this argument is derived from the Laffer Curve, named after the economist Arthur B. Laffer. See Victor A. Canto, Douglas H. Joines, and Arthur B. Laffer, *Foundations of Supply Side Economics* (New York: Academic Press, 1983).

11. John J. Harrigan, *Politics and Policy in States and Communities*, 5th ed. (New York: HarperCollins, 1994), 70–75.

12. Elizabeth G. Hill, Legislative Analyst's Office, *California's Tax System: A Primer*, http://www.lao.ca.gov/2007/tax_primer/tax_primer_040907.pdf (accessed February 1, 2015).

13. These firms are Standard and Poor's, Moody's, and Fitch.

14. Tami Luhby, "California's Brown Plans $12.5 billion in Cuts," *CNN Money. com*, http://money.cnn.com/2011/01/10/news/economy/California_budget_brown/ index.htm (accessed February 2, 2015).

15. Steven Greenhut, "Smoke and Mirrors in Sacramento," *City Journal*, http:// www.city-journal.org/2010/eon1026sg.html (accessed February 2, 2015).

16. David Lyon, "California's Deficit Defies Partisan Blame: Budget's Pendulum-Like Swings Are Hard to Manage," *Public Policy Institute of California*, http://www .ppic.org/main/commentary.asp?i=255 (accessed February 2, 2015).

17. Greenhut, "Smoke and Mirrors"; See also Dan Balz, "In California's Budget Crisis, Lessons for the Rest of Us?" *Washington Post*, http://voices.washingtonpost .com/44/2009/07/21/in_californias_budget_crisis_l.html (accessed February 2, 2015).

18. "What Caused the Budget Mess?" *Reason Foundation*, http://reason.org/news/ show/1007039.html (accessed February 2, 2015).

19. Dan Walters, "Brown's Budget Faces the State's Ugly Facts," http://www.ocreg ister.com/articles/brown-283655-california-taxes.html (accessed February 2, 2015).

20. Greenhut, "Smoke and Mirrors."

Chapter 10. Local Government

1. Alexis de Tocqueville, *Democracy in America*, trans., ed., and with an introduction by Harvey C. Mansfield and Delba Winthrop (Chicago: University of Chicago Press, 2000), 57.

2. Tocqueville, *Democracy in America*, 531.

3. California League of Cities, http://www.cacities.org/Resources/Learn-About -Cities (accessed January 18, 2015).

4. The nature of the relationship between elected officials and their constituents has been broken down by political scholars into two major categories: trustee and delegate. A trustee sees the role of the representative as one who is expected to take into account the views of the constituency but who, in the end, will perform his or her duty to exercise independent judgment on policy matters. A delegate is a representative who views the role as one who implements the will of his or her constituents. See Edmund Burke, *Works* (Boston: Little, Brown, 1986; first published 1866), vol. 2, 95–96; Walter Lippmann, *The Public Philosophy* (Boston: Little, Brown, 1955); John C. Wahlke et al., *The Legislative System* (New York: Wiley, 1962); Roger H. Davidson, *The Role of the Congressman* (New York: Pegasus, 1969); and Charles G. Bell and Charles M. Price, "Pre-Legislative Sources of Representational Roles," *Midwest Journal of Political Science* 13 (1969): 254–70.

5. Robert L. Linberry and Edmund P. Fowler, "Reformism and Public Policies in American Cities," *American Political Science Review* 61 (1967): 701–16.

6. The Lakewood Plan is attractive to cities because it provides them with the means to receive cost-effective services.

7. The U.S. Census Bureau defines a special district according to the following three criteria: existence of an organized entity, governmental character, and substantial autonomy. See U.S. Bureau of the Census, *1982 Census of Governments* 4, no. 2 (1982): vi.

8. *Statistical Abstract of the United States*, "Number of Local Governments, by Type," http://www.census.gov/compendia/statab/2011/tables/11s0427.pdf (accessed February 2, 2015).

9. *Statistical Abstract of the United States*, "Number of Local Governments, by Type."

10. Jean Ross, "Perspectives on Proposition 13: Flawed Reform," *California Journal* 28 (1997): 26.

11. Ann O'M. Bowman and Richard C. Kearney, *State and Local Government: The Essentials* (Boston: Houghton-Mifflin Company, 2003), 276–82.

12. See Secretary of State, *Official Voter Information Guide for the General Election* (Sacramento, 2000), 33–37.

13. A. G. Block and Charles Price, "Local Government," *California Government and Politics Annual* (Sacramento: StateNet, 1999), 68.

14. *Statistical Abstract of the United States*, "Number of Local Governments, by Type."

15. Nancy Burns, *The Formation of American Local Governments* (New York: Oxford University Press, 1994), 11.

16. Douglas R. Porter et al., *Special Districts* (Washington, D.C.: Urban Land Institute, 1992), 32.

17. John C. Bollens, *Special District Governments in the United States* (Berkeley: University of California Press, 1957); and Advisory Commission on Intergovernmental Relations, *The Problems of Special Districts in American Government* (Washington, D.C., 1964).

18. Charles Tiebout, "A Pure Theory of Local Government Expenditures," *Journal of Political Economy* 64 (1956): 416–24; and Robert Bisch and Vincent Ostrom, *Understanding Urban Government: Metropolitan Reform Reconsidered* (Washington, D.C.: AEI Press, 1979).

19. For a more thorough analysis of the bureaucratic element of this phenomenon, see Robert K. Merton, "Bureaucratic Structure and Personality," *Social Forces* 18 (1940): 560–68.

20. Robert B. Hawkins Jr., *Self Government by District: Myth and Reality* (Stanford, CA: Hoover Institution Press, 1976).

21. Hawkins, *Self Government*, 52.

22. Hawkins, *Self Government*, 52.

23. Tocqueville, *Democracy in America*, 67.

Epilogue

1. Tocqueville, *Democracy in America*, 676.

Bibliography

Advisory Commission on Intergovernmental Relations. *The Problems of Special Districts in American Government.* Washington, D.C.: ACIR, 1964.

Adler, Ben. "It's Gut-and-Amend Time at the Capitol," Capital Public Radio, http://www.capradio.org/articles/2014/08/27/its-gut-and-amend-time-at-the-capitol/ (accessed February 1, 2015)

Ainsworth, Bill. "Astroturf Lobbying." *California Government and Politics Annual: 1998–1999.* Sacramento: StateNet, 1998, 39–40.

Alschuler, Alan W. *Law without Values: The Life, Work, and Legacy of Justice Holmes.* Chicago: University of Chicago Press, 2000.

Ambrose, Stephen E. *Nothing Like It in the World: The Men Who Built the Transcontinental Railroad 1863–1869.* New York: Simon & Schuster, 2000.

American Academy of Pediatrics v. Lungen (1997) 16 Cal. 4th 307.

American Society for Public Administration. "Bell Tolls for Effective Communication of Compensation." 2010. http://aspanational.wordpress.com/2010/09/30/bell-tolls -for-effective-communication-of-compensation/ (accessed January 6, 2011).

Anderson, Terry L., and P. J. Hill. "The Evolution of Property Rights: A Study of the American West," *Journal of Law and Economics* 28, no. 1 (April 1975): 163–79.

———. "An American Experiment in Anarcho-Capitalism: The *Not* So Wild, Wild West." *Journal of Libertarian Studies* 3, no. 1 (Spring 1979): 9–28.

Aristotle, *The Politics.* Translated with introduction, notes, and glossary by Carnes Lord. Chicago: University of Chicago Press, 1984.

Aristotle. *The Politics.* Translated with introduction and notes by Peter L. Phillips Simpson. Chapel Hill: University of North Carolina, 1997.

"Assembly." *California Journal* 31, no. 2 (2000): 31–58.

Baker, Ross K. "Conservatives Wrongly Seek 'Government by Tantrum.'" *USA Today.* August 11, 2003. 11A.

Bakke v. Regents of the University of California (1976) 18 Cal. 3d 34.

Baldassare, Mark. *California in the New Millennium.* Berkeley: University of California Press, 2000.

Ball, Howard. *The Bakke Case: Race, Education, and Affirmative Action.* Lawrence: University Press of Kansas, 2000.

Balz, Dan. "In California's Budget Crisis, Lessons for the Rest of Us?" *Washington Post,* http://voices.washingtonpost.com/44/2009/07/21/in_californias_budget_crisis_l.html (accessed February 2, 2015).

Barrilleaux, Charles. "Governors, Bureaus, and State Policymaking." *State and Local Government Review* 21, no. 1 (1989): 53–59.

BBC News, "Protesters Block Migrant Busses in California," http://www.bbc.com/news/world-us-canada-28121198 (accessed January 25, 2015).

Beard, Charles. *An Economic Interpretation of the Constitution of the United States.* New York: Macmillan, 1913.

Bell, Charles G., and Charles M. Price. "Pre-Legislative Sources of Representational Roles." *Midwest Journal of Political Science* 13 (1969): 254–70.

Bellah, Robert et al. *Habits of the Heart.* Berkeley: University of California, 1985.

Bellandi, Deanna. "California Appeals Sutter-Summit Merger Ruling." *Modern Healthcare* 31 (January 2000): 4.

Belz, Herman. "Popular Sovereignty, The Right of Revolution, and California Statehood," 3–31 in *The California Republic,* edited by Brian P. Janiskee and Ken Masugi. Lanham, MD: Rowman & Littlefield, 2004.

Berkman, Michael, and James Eisenstein. "State Legislators as Congressional Candidates." *Political Research Quarterly* 52, no. 3 (1999): 481–98.

Bernstein, Sharon, and Robert A. Rosenblatt. "Average HMO Medicare Rate Set to Double." *Los Angeles Times* (September 16, 2000): 1.

Berthelsen, Christian. "Senate Committee Revives Same-Sex Marriage Bill." *San Francisco Chronicle* (July 13, 2005): B1.

Bessette, Joseph M. *The Mild Voice of Reason.* Chicago: University of Chicago Press, 1994.

BeVier, Michael J. *Politics Backstage.* Philadelphia: Temple University Press, 1979.

Bisch, Robert, and Vincent Ostrom. *Understanding Urban Government: Metropolitan Reform Reconsidered.* Washington, D.C.: AEI Press, 1979.

Block, A. G., and Charles M. Price, eds. *California Government and Politics Annual: 1998–1999.* Sacramento, CA: StateNet Publications, 1998.

———. "Local Government." In *California Government and Politics Annual,* edited by A. G. Block and Charles M. Price. Sacramento, CA: StateNet Publications, 1999, 68.

Bollens, John C. *Special District Governments in the United States.* Berkeley: University of California Press, 1957.

Bottom, William P., Cheryl L. Eavey, Gary J. Miller, and Jennifer Nicoll Victor. "The Institutional Effect on Majority Rule Instability: Bicameralism in Spatial Policy Decisions." *American Journal of Political Science* 44, no. 3 (2000): 523–40.

Brinkerhoff, Noel. "The Strangest of Bedfellows." *California Journal* 31 (May 2000): 24–28.

Broder, David S. "Repairing California Government." *Washington Post*, October 8, 2003. A29.

Bryce, James. *The American Commonwealth*, vol. 2. Indianapolis: Liberty Fund Press, 1995.

Buckley v. Valeo (1976) 425 U.S. 946.

Burns, Nancy. *The Formation of American Local Governments*. New York: Oxford University Press, 1994.

Burke, Edmund. *Works*. Boston: Little, Brown & Company, 1986.

Burns, James MacGregor, et al. *State and Local Politics*, 8th ed. Upper Saddle River, NJ: Prentice-Hall, 1996, 114–16.

Bush v. Gore (2000) 531 U.S. 98.

Cain, Bruce E., and Roger G. Noll, eds. *Constitutional Reform in California*. Berkeley: University of California, Institute of Governmental Studies Press, 1995.

California Citizens Compensation Commission. "Salaries of Elected Officials." http://www.dpa.ca.gov/cccc/salaries/main.htm (accessed January 18, 2015).

California Constitution Revision Commission. *Final Report and Recommendations to the Governor and the Legislature*. Sacramento: State of California, 1996.

California Democratic Party v. Jones (2000) 530 U.S. 567.

California Courts, http://www.courts.ca.gov/2948.htm (accessed January 18, 2015).

———. Fact Sheet. http://www.courts.ca.gov/documents/Calif_Judicial_Branch.pdf (accessed 19 January 2015).

———. Introduction. Court Statistics Report 2012–2013. California Courts, "Introduction," Court Statistics Report 2012–2013, http://www.courts.ca.gov/documents/2014-Court-Statistics-Report-Introduction.pdf (accessed January 18, 2015).

California League of Cities. http://www.cacities.org/Resources/Learn-About-Cities (accessed January 18, 2015).

California, Lieutenant Governor. http://www.ltg.ca.gov/m_about.html (accessed February 1, 2015).

California, State of. http://www.ca.gov/index.asp (accessed February 2, 2015).

California Supreme Court. http://www.courts.ca.gov/documents/2007_Supreme_Court_Booklet_withInserts.pdf (accessed February 2, 2015).

Carey, John M., Richard G. Niemi, and Lynda W. Powell. "Incumbency and the Probability of Reelection in State Legislative Elections." *Journal of Politics* 62 (August 2000): 671–700.

Carlton, Jim. "Gay Activists Boycott Backers of Prop. 8," *Wall Street Journal* http://online.wsj.com/article/SB123033766467736451.html (accessed February 2, 2015).

CBS News. "Bell City Council to Hold Recall Election." 2010. http://www.cbsnews.com/stories/2010/11/02/national/main7013479.shtml (accessed January 6, 2011).

CBS News, Los Angeles. "Former Bell City Councilman Sentenced to Probation, 1 Year in Jail," http://losangeles.cbslocal.com/2014/07/11/former-bell-city-councilman-sentenced-to-probation-1-year-in-jail/ (accessed January 29, 2015).

Census Bureau of the, United States. *Census of Governments*. Washington, D.C.: United States Government Printing Office, 1982. http://www.ceousa.org/content/blogcategory/78/100/ (accessed January 19, 2011).

Center for Investigative Reporting. http://californiawatch.org/dailyreport/despite-di versity-efforts-uc-minority-enrollment-down-prop-209-15031 (accessed January 25, 2015).

Chavez, Lydia. *The Color Bind: California's Battle to End Affirmative Action.* Berkeley: University of California Press, 1998.

Chokshi, Niraj. "These 5 Maps Show Unions Are Losing Ground in the States," *Washington Post,* http://www.washingtonpost.com/blogs/govbeat/wp/2014/01/27/ these-5-maps-show-unions-are-losing-ground-in-the-states/ (accessed January 31, 2015).

Citizens Redistricting Commission, http://wedrawthelines.ca.gov/commission.html (accessed 1 February 2015).

Citizens United v. FEC (2010) 558 U.S. 310.

Citrin, Jack, and Benjamin Highton. *How Race, Ethnicity, and Immigration Shape the California Electorate.* San Francisco: Public Policy Institute of California, 2002.

Clement, Scott. "Do Americans Want to Stop Obama's Immigration Move? Yes and No." *Washington Post,* http://www.washingtonpost.com/blogs/the-fix/ wp/2015/01/20/do-people-want-to-stop-obamas-immigration-move-yes-and-no/ (accessed January 25, 2015).

Codevilla, Angelo. *The Character of Nations: How Politics Makes and Breaks Prosperity, Family, and Civility.* New York: HarperCollins, Basic Books, 1997.

Commager, Henry Steele, ed. *Documents of American History.* Englewood Cliffs, NJ: Prentice- Hall, 1973.

Connerly, Ward. *Creating Equal: My Fight against Race Preferences.* San Francisco: Encounter Books, 2000.

Cook, Marian Miner. Speech, Claremont McKenna College, Claremont, California, October 23, 2003.

Coolican, J. Patrick "City of Bell Officials Arrested." *LA Weekly.* 2010. http://blogs. laweekly.com/informer/2010/09/city_of_bell_officials_arreste.php# (accessed February 2, 2015).

Council of State Governments. *The Book of the States, 2000–2001.* Lexington, KY: Council of State Governments, 2000.

——. http://knowledgecenter.csg.org/kc/content/book-states-2010-chapter-1-state -constitutions (accessed January 20, 2015).

Coupal, Jonathon. "Perspectives on Proposition 13: Fairness for Taxpayers." *California Journal* 28 (1997): 27.

Craft, Cynthia H. "The Economic Silver Lining to Gun Laws." *California Journal* 31 (March 2000): 18–22.

Croly, Herbert. *The Promise of American Life.* New York: Capricorn, 1964.

C-SPAN. Arnold Schwarzenegger, State of the State Address, January 6, 2004, http:// www.c-span.org/video/?179801-1/california-state-state-address (accessed February 2, 2015).

Daily News (Los Angeles). "Rain's Not the Only Thing Soaking Us." December 2010, 1(A).

Davidson, Roger H. *The Role of the Congressman.* New York: Pegasus, 1969.

De Atley, Richard K. "How to Become a Judge?" *The Press-Enterprise* (Riverside, CA) (July 31, 2006): B1.

Department of Finance, California. http://www.dof.ca.gov/HTML/FS_DATA/Latest EconData/documents/BBRANK.XLS (accessed January 20, 2015).

———. www.dof.ca.gov/fisa/bag/process.htm (accessed February 1, 2015).

Dewey, John. *The Public and Its Problems.* Chicago: Swallow Press, 1927.

Diamond, Martin. *The Founding of the Democratic Republic.* Itasca, IL: F. E. Peacock, 1981.

DiClerico, Robert. *Political Parties, Campaigns and Elections.* Upper Saddle River, NJ: Prentice-Hall, 2000.

Douglass, John Aubrey. *The California Idea and American Higher Education.* Stanford, CA: Stanford University Press, 2000.

Dinan, John. "Framing a Peoples' Government: State Constitution-Making in the Progressive Era." *Rutgers Law Journal* 30 (1999): 933–85.

Downs, Anthony. "Up and Down with Ecology: The 'Issue Attention Cycle.'" *The Public Interest* 28 (1972): 38–50.

Dred Scott v. Sanford (1857) 60 U.S. 393.

Drucker, David M. "Demos Moving to Satisfy Schwarzenegger on SB 60." *Inland Valley Bulletin.* October 28, 2003. A11.

Dubois, Phillip L. *Lawmaking by Initiative.* New York: Agathon, 1998.

Eck, Diana L. *A New Religious America: How a "Christian Country" Has Become the World's Most Religiously Diverse Nation.* San Francisco: Harper San Francisco, 2001.

Economist. "Suddenly Brown's a Winner." (May 22, 1976): 33.

Ehrenfreund, Max "Your Complete Guide to Obama's Immigration Executive Action," *Washington Post,* http://www.washingtonpost.com/blogs/wonkblog/wp/2014/11/19/your-complete-guide-to-obamas-immigration-order/ (accessed January 22, 2015).

Elias, Thomas D. "Will Arnold Try to End Gut-Amend?" *Daily News of Los Angeles* (August 30, 2004): N13.

Erler, Edward, J. *The American Polity: Essays on the Theory and Practice of Constitutional Government.* Washington, D.C.: Crane Russak, 1991.

———. "Californians and Their Constitution: Progressivism, Direct Democracy, and the Administrative State." pp. 97–126 in *The California Republic*, edited by Brian P. Janiskee and Ken Masugi. Lanham, MD: Rowman & Littlefield, 2004.

Erler, Edward J., Thomas G. West, and John Marini. *The Founders on Citizenship and Immigration: Principles and Challenges in America.* Lanham, MD: Rowman & Littlefield, 2007.

Fair Political Practices Commission, California. *Big Money Talks: California's Billion Dollar Club.* 2010. http://www.fppc.ca.gov/reports/Report31110.pdf (accessed January 29, 2015), 10.

Fehrenbacher, Don E. *The Dred Scott Case: Its Significance in American Law and Politics.* New York: Oxford University Press, 1975.

———. *Slavery, Law, and Politics: The Dred Scott Case in Historical Perspective.* New York: Oxford University Press, 1981.

Fehrenbacher, Don, and Norman Tutorow. *California: An Illustrated History.* New York: D. Van Nostrand, 1968.

Fenno, Richard F., Jr. *Homestyle.* Boston: Little, Brown, 1978.

Finnegan, Michael. "Neel Kashkari Spent More Than Jerry Brown on Governor's Race," *Los Angeles Times* http://www.latimes.com/local/political/la-me-pc-kash kari-brown-campaign-spending-20150130-story.html (accessed February 1, 2015).

Fiorina, Morris. *Divided Government.* 2nd ed. New York: Allyn and Bacon, 1996.

Folkenflik, David. "How *The L.A. Times* Broke the Bell Corruption Story." *NPR.* 2010. http://www.npr.org/templates/story/story.php?storyId=130108851 (accessed January 6, 2011).

Fox, Joel. "California's Problem Isn't Prop. 13." *Los Angeles Times*, May 30, 2003. B7.

Fuchs, Lawrence H. *The American Kaleidoscope: Race, Ethnicity, and the Civic Culture.* Hanover: University Press of New England, 1990.

Fukuyama, Francis. *The Great Disruption: Human Nature and the Reconstitution of Social Order.* New York: Touchstone Books, 1999.

Galderisi, Peter F., ed. *Divided Government: Change, Uncertainty, and the Constitutional Order.* Lanham, MD: Rowman & Littlefield, 1996.

Garrison, Jessica, and Joanna Lin. "Prop. 8 Protesters Target Mormon Temple in Westwood." *Los Angeles Times*, http://www.latimes.com/news/local/la-me-pro test7-2008nov07,0,3827549.story (accessed February 2, 2015).

Geer, John G., ed. *Politicians and Party Politics.* Baltimore: Johns Hopkins University Press, 2000.

Germond, Jack, and Jules Witcover. "Wilson's Pledge Haunted His Candidacy." *The National Journal* 27 (October 1995): 2495.

Getlin, Josh. "Regarding the Media; for Whom the Polls Toll—the Candidate Who's Trailing." *Los Angeles Times* (September 18, 2000): E1.

Glazer, Nathan. *We Are All Multiculturalists Now.* Cambridge, MA: Harvard University Press, 1997.

Goldman, Peter Thomas, et al. "How Tight Can It Get?" *Newsweek* (July 12, 1976): 16.

Gordon, Larry. "UC leases housing at $9,950 a month for president Napolitano," *Los Angeles Times*, http://articles.latimes.com/2013/sep/16/local/la-me-ln-uc -rental-20130916 (accessed January 18, 2015).

Gottlieb, Jeff, and Reuben Vines. "Is a City Manager Worth $800,000?." *Los Angeles Times.* 2010. http://www.latimes.com/news/local/la-me-bell-sal ary-20100715,0,7352605.story (accessed January 6, 2011).

Governor's Budget. "Enacted Budget Detail." http://www.ebudget.ca.gov/2013-14/ Enacted/agencies.html (accessed January 18, 2015).

———. "Enacted Budget Summary" http://www.ebudget.ca.gov/2013-14/pdf/Enacted/ BudgetSummary/SummaryCharts.pdf (accessed January 18, 2015).

Greenhut, Steven. "Smoke and Mirrors in Sacramento." *City Journal*, http://www .city-journal.org/2010/eon1026sg.html (accessed February 2, 2015).

Grodin, Joseph R. *In Pursuit of Justice: Reflections of a State Supreme Court Justice.* Foreword by Justice William J. Brennan, Jr. Berkeley: University of California Press, 1989.

Grofman, Bernard, ed. *Race and Redistricting in the 1990s.* New York: Agathon, 1999.

"Gut and Amend." *The San Diego Union-Tribune* (August 18, 2004): B8.

Halper, Evan. "State Triples Vehicle Fees." *Los Angeles Times*, June 21, 2003. B1.

Hamilton, Alexander, James Madison, and John Jay. *The Federalist Papers.* Edited by Clinton Rossiter with introduction and notes by Charles R. Kesler. New York: Penguin, Mentor Books, 1999.

Hammond, Thomas H., and Gary J. Miller. "The Core of the Constitution." *American Political Science Review* 81 (1987): 1155–74.

Hanson, Victor Davis. *The Land Was Everything.* New York: Free Press, 2000.

———. *Mexifornia: A State of Becoming.* San Francisco: Encounter Books, 2003.

———. "Two Californias." *National Review Online.* http://www.nationalreview.com/articles/255320/two-californias-victor-davis-hanson (accessed January 18, 2011).

Harrigan, John J. *Politics and Policy in States and Communities.* 5th ed. New York: Harper Collins, 1994.

Hawkins, Robert B. Jr. *Self Government by District: Myth and Reality.* Stanford, CA: Hoover Institution Press, 1976.

Hayward, Steven F. *The Age of Reagan, 1964–1980: The Fall of the Old Liberal Order.* New York: Prima Publishing, 2001.

———. "Ronald Reagan and the Transformation of Modern California." pp. 237–53 in *The California Republic,* edited by Brian P. Janiskee and Ken Masugi. Lanham, MD: Rowman & Littlefield, 2004.

———. *The Age of Reagan: The Conservative Counterrevolution: 1980–1989.* New York: Crown Forum, 2009.

Helfand, Duke, and Robert J. Lopez. "Mayor to Name 31-year Veteran Douglas Barry as Acting Chief Today." *Los Angeles Times* (December 4, 2006): A1.

Hibbing, John R. "Legislative Careers: Why and How We Should Study Them." *Legislative Studies Quarterly* 24, no. 2 (1999): 149–71.

Hill, Elizabeth G. *California's Tax System: A Primer,* http://www.lao.ca.gov/2007/tax_primer/tax_primer_040907.pdf (accessed February 1, 2015).

Hirsch, Barry, and David Macpherson. http://www.unionstats.com/ (accessed January 31, 2015).

Hollingsworth v. *Perry* (2013) 570 U.S. ___.

"How Much Does Your City Pay Its Manager? Look Here." 2010. *San Francisco Chronicle,* http://www.sfgate.com/cgi-bin/blogs/nov05election/detail?entry_id=72074 (accessed January 6, 2011).

Hubler, Shawn. "Truth and Consequences for the LAPD." *Los Angeles Times* (September 18, 2000): B1.

Huntington, Samuel. "The Special Case of Mexican Immigration: Why Mexico Is a Problem." *The American Enterprise* (December 2000): 22.

In re Marriage Cases. 43 Cal.4th 757 (2008) [Cal.Rptr.3d 683, 183 P.3d 384 76].

Ingraham, Patricia Wallace. *The Foundation of Merit: Public Service in American Democracy.* Baltimore: Johns Hopkins University Press, 1995.

Inland Valley Daily Bulletin. "Disclosure Can Check Influence." (July 22, 2010). *Lexis/Nexis Academic.* http://www.lexisnexis.com/news/ (accessed January 8, 2010).

"In the Running for California Governor." *Los Angeles Times*, August 10, 2003, A32.

Jaffa, Harry V. "The Nature and Origin of the American Party System." In *Equality and Liberty*. New York, Oxford University Press, 1965, 3–41.

———. *Crisis of the House Divided: An Interpretation of the Issues in the Lincoln-Douglas Debates*. Chicago: University of Chicago Press, 1982.

———. *American Conservatism and the American Founding*. Durham, NC: Carolina Academic Press, 1984.

———. *A New Birth of Freedom: Abraham Lincoln and the Coming of the Civil War*. Lanham, MD: Rowman & Littlefield, 2000.

Janiskee, Brian P. "The United States Presidential Election of 2000: The Prospects for Controversy." *Talking Politics: The Journal of the Politics Association* 12 (Winter 2000): 337–42.

Janiskee, Brian P., and Edward J. Erler. "Crime, Punishment and *Romero:* An Analysis of the Case Against California's Three Strikes Law." *Duquesne Law Review* 39 (Fall 2000): 43–65.

Janiskee, Brian P., and Ken Masugi, ed. *The California Republic*. Lanham, MD: Rowman & Littlefield, 2004.

Jefferson, Thomas. "First Inaugural Address." March 4, 1801. In *Jefferson*. Edited by Merrill Peterson. New York: Library of America, 1984.

King, James D. "Changes in Professionalism in U.S. State Legislatures." *Legislative Studies Quarterly* 25, no. 2 (2000): 327–43.

Kingdon, John W. *Congressmen's Voting Decisions*. 3rd ed. Ann Arbor: University of Michigan Press, 1989.

Knoll, Corina. "Former Bell Councilwoman Teresa Jacobo Gets Two-Year Prison Sentence," *Los Angeles Times*, http://www.latimes.com/local/la-me-bell-sentence -20140726-story.html (accessed January 29, 2015).

Knoll, Corina. "Final Bell Council Member Sentenced," *Los Angeles Times*, http:// www.latimes.com/local/politics/la-me-0802-bell-finale-20140802-story.html (accessed January 29, 2015).

Knoll, Corina, and Jeff Gottlieb. "Rizzo Gets 12 Years in Prison, Marking End to Scandal That Rocked Bell," *Los Angeles Times*, http://www.latimes.com/local/ lanow/la-me-ln-rizzo-set-to-be-sentenced--20140415-story.html (accessed January 29, 2015).

Kotkin, Joel. http://www.joelkotkin.com (accessed February 2, 2015).

Laffer, Arthur B., Victor A. Canto, and Douglas H. Joines. *Foundations of Supply Side Economics*. New York: Academic Press, 1983.

League of Women Voters. *Guide to California Government*. Sacramento: League of Women Voters Education Fund, 1992.

Legislative Analyst's Office, California Legislature. *CAL Facts*. Sacramento: Legislative Analyst's Office, 2000.

———. *Legislative Analyst's Office*. "Proposition 14." 2010, http://www.lao.ca.gov/bal lot/2010/14_06_2010.aspx (accessed February 2, 2015).

———. *Legislative Analyst's Office*, http://www.lao.ca.gov/ballot/2013/130771.aspx (accessed January 15, 2015).

———. "The 2013–14 Budget: California Spending Plan," http://lao.ca.gov/reports/2013/ bud/spending-plan/spending-plan-073013.aspx (accessed January 18, 2015).

Les, Kathleen. "Business's Big Guns." *California Government and Politics Annual 1998–1999.* Sacramento: StateNet, 1999: 43–44.

———. "Making the Grade at Hertzberg U." *California Journal* 31 (2000): 32–39

———. "Labor Toils Mightily for a Select Few." *California Journal* 31 (2000): 46–49.

Linberry, Robert L., and Edmund P. Fowler, "Reformism and Public Policies in American Cities." *American Political Science Review* 61 (1967): 701–16.

Lincoln, Abraham. June 26, 1857. In *The Collected Works of Abraham,* vol. 2. Edited by Roy P. Basler. New Brunswick, NJ: Rutgers University Press, 1953, 400–401.

———. "Address before the Wisconsin State Agricultural Society, Milwaukee, Wisconsin." September 30, 1859. In *Collected Works,* vol. 3. New Brunswick, NJ: Rutgers University Press, 1953.

Lippmann, Walter. *The Public Philosophy.* Boston: Little, Brown and Company, 1955.

Lloyd, Gordon. "Nature and Convention in the Creation of the 1849 California Constitution."

Lopez, Steve. "Meg Whitman Spent $50 for Each Vote She Got. Is That an Outrageous Extravagance?" 2010. http://latimesblogs.latimes.com/lanow/2010/11/steve-lopez-meg-whitman-spent-50-for-each-vote-she-got-is-that-an-outrageous-extravagance.html (accessed February 2, 2015).

Lower, Richard Coke. *A Bloc of One: the Political Career of Hiram W. Johnson.* Stanford, CA: Stanford University Press, 1993.

Lucas, Greg, and Matthew Yi. "At Session-end, Old Bills Take on Brand New Lives." *San Francisco Chronicle* (August 31, 2006): B2.

Luhby, Tami. "California's Brown Plans $12.5 Billion in Cuts." *CNN Money.com,* http://money.cnn.com/2011/01/10/news/economy/California_budget_brown/index.htm (accessed February 2, 2015).

Mansell, Stephen. *California in Context: A 50 State Comparison of State Legislatures.* Claremont, CA: Rose Institute, 1999.

Marini, John. *The Politics of Budget Control: Congress, the Presidency, and the Growth of the Administrative State.* Washington, D.C.: Crane Russak, 1991.

Marini, John, and Ken Masugi, eds. *The Progressive Revolution in Politics and Political Science.* Lanham, MD: Rowman & Littlefield, 2005.

Martin, Mark, Carla Marinucci, and Lynda Gledhill. "The Special Election; Californians Say No to Schwarzenegger." *San Francisco Chronicle* (November 9, 2005): A1.

Martinez, Michael. "Voters Recall Councilmen in Scandal-plagued California City," *CNN* http://www.cnn.com/2011/CRIME/03/10/california.bell.scandal/ (accessed January 29, 2015).

May, Meredith. "Little Improvement in Dropout Rates from California Schools." *San Francisco Chronicle* (June 9, 2000): A3.

Mayer, Gerald. "Union Membership Trends in the United States," Cornell University ILR School, http://digitalcommons.ilr.cornell.edu/cgi/viewcontent.cgi?article=1176&context=key_workplace (accessed January 31, 2015), 12.

Mayhew, David. *Divided We Govern.* New Haven, CT: Yale University Press, 1991.

McClain, Charles J. *In Search of Equality: The Chinese Struggle against Discrimination in Nineteenth-Century America.* Berkeley: University of California Press, 1994.

McCulloch v. Maryland (1819) 17 U.S. 316.

McGreevy, Patrick. "Senate Leader Reshuffles Committee Chairs," *Los Angeles Times*, http://latimesblogs.latimes.com/california-politics/2011/01/senate-leader-reshuffles-committee-chairs.html (accessed February 2, 2015).

McWilliams, Carey. *California: The Great Exception*. Foreword by Lewis H. Lapham. Berkeley: University of California, 1999; originally published 1949.

Merton, Robert K. "Bureaucratic Structure and Personality." *Social Forces* 18 (1940): 560–68.

Milkis, Sidney M. *Theodore Roosevelt, the Progressive Party, and the Transformation of American Democracy*. Lawrence: University Press of Kansas, 2009.

Morehouse, Sarah McCally. *The Governor as Party Leader*. Ann Arbor: University of Michigan Press, 1998.

Murphy, Katy. "California's Affirmative Action Ban Bolstered by Supreme Court Ruling," *San Jose Mercury News*, http://www.mercurynews.com/education/ci_25617295/californias-affirmative-action-ban-bolstered-by-supreme-court (accessed January 25, 2015).

Mowry, George E. *The California Progressives*. Chicago: Quadrangle, 1963.

National Archives. http://www.archives.gov/exhibits/charters/constitution_q_and_a.html (accessed January 20, 2015).

National Conference of State Legislatures. "Full and Part-Time Legislatures." http://www.ncsl.org/research/about-state-legislatures/full-and-part-time-legislatures.aspx (accessed February 1, 2015).

———. "Initiative, Referendum, and Recall," http://www.ncsl.org/research/elections-and-campaigns/initiative-referendum-and-recall-overview.aspx (accessed February 2, 2015).

———. http://www.ncsl.org/research/about-state-legislatures/2014-ncsl-legislator-salary-and-per-diem-table.aspx (accessed February 1, 2015).

———. http://www.ncsl.org/research/about-state-legislatures/legislative-session-length.aspx (accessed February 1, 2015).

Nichols, Stephen M. "State Referendum Voting, Ballot Roll-Off, and the Effect of New Electoral Technology." *State and Local Government Review* 30 (Spring 1998): 106–13.

Nixon v. Shrink Missouri Government PAC (2000) 528 U.S. 377.

Norris, Frank. *The Octopus: A Story of California*. New York: New American Library, Signet Classics, 1964.

Olson, Mancur, Jr. *The Logic of Collective Action*. New York: Schocken, 1968.

Ornstein, Norman, Thomas Mann, and Michael Malbin. *Vital Statistics on Congress, 1993–1994*. Washington, D.C.: Congressional Quarterly Press, 1994.

Pestritto, Ronald J. *Woodrow Wilson and the Roots of Modern Liberalism*. Lanham, MD: Rowman & Littlefield, 2005.

Pitney, John J. "Nixon, California, and American Politics." pp. 219–35 in *The California Republic*, edited by Brian P. Janiskee and Ken Masugi. Lanham, MD: Rowman & Littlefield, 204.

Plunkitt, George Washington. *Plunkitt of Tammany Hall*, as recorded by William L. Riordon. New York: E. P. Dutton, 1963.

Political Reform Division, State of California. http://www.sos.ca.gov/prd/ (accessed January 6, 2011).

Porter, Douglas R., Ben C. In *Special Districts*. Edited by Susan Jakubiak and Richard B. Peiser. Washington, D.C.: Urban Land Institute, 1992.

"Propositions" *California Journal* 31 (February 2000): 59–71.

Public Policy Institute of California. "California's Likely Voters," http://www.ppic.org/main/publication_show.asp?i=255 (accessed January 20, 2015).

———. "California's Deficit Defies Partisan Blame: Budget's Pendulum-Like Swings are Hard to Manage." http://www.ppic.org/main/commentary.asp?i=255 (accessed January 15, 2011).

Putnam, Robert D. *Bowling Alone: The Collapse and Revival of American Community*. New York: Simon & Schuster, 2000.

Raven v. Deukmejian (1990) 52 Cal. 3d 336.

Reason Foundation. "What Caused the Budget Mess?" http://reason.org/news/show/1007039.html (accessed February 2, 2015).

Regents of the University of California v. Bakke (1978) 438 U.S. 912.

Rodriguez, Richard. *Days of Obligation: Arguments with My Mexican Father*. New York: Viking, 1992.

Roe v. Wade (1973) 410 U.S. 113.

Rohrbough, Malcolm J. *Days of Gold: The California Gold Rush and the American Nation*. Berkeley: University of California Press, 1997.

Rosenthal, Alan. *The Decline of Representative Democracy*. Washington, D.C.: Congressional Quarterly Press, 1997.

Ross, Jean. "Perspectives on Proposition 13: Flawed Reform." *California Journal* 28 (1997): 26.

Rough and Tumble. rtumble.com (accessed 17 January 2011).

Rush, Mark, ed. *Voting Rights and Redistricting in the United States*. Westport, CT: Greenwood, 1999.

Sabato, Larry J. "Tyranny of the Mob Rules in California." *Los Angeles Times*. August 19, 2003, B13.

Sacramento Bee. "Pérez Announces Leadership and Committee Assignments," 2010. http://blogs.sacbee.com/capitolalertlatest/2010/12/perez-announces-dem-leadership.html (accessed January 9, 2011).

Samuelson, Robert J. "Who Cares How Rich Bill Gates Is?" *Washington Post* (May 2, 2001): A21.

———. "Candor on Immigration." *Washington Post* (June 8, 2005): A21.

Schattschneider, E. E. *The Semi-Sovereign People*. New York: Holt, Rinehart, and Winston, 1960.

Schwartz, Stephen. *From West to East: California and the Making of the American Mind*. New York: Free Press, 1998.

Scott, Steve. "And They're Off!" *California Journal* 31 (February 2000): 6–8.

———. "Davis, the Political Powerhouse." *California Journal* 21 (August 2000): 28–31.

Seattle Government. http://www.seattle.gov/financedepartment/cpi/documents/US_CPI_History_- -_Annual_000.pdf (accessed February 2, 2015).

Secretary of State, Office of the, California. *Statement of the Vote, November 3, 1998.* Sacramento: State of California, 1998.

———. "Proposition 209: Text of Proposed Law," http://vote96.sos.ca.gov/html/BP/209text.htm (accessed January 25, 2015).

———. http://www.sos.ca.gov/elections/elections_t.htm (accessed January 6, 2011).

———. http://elections.cdn.sos.ca.gov/sov/2003-special/sov-complete.pdf (accessed 1 February 2015).

———. "Summary of Qualifications and Requirements for Independent Nomination for the Offices of Governor and Lieutenant Governor." http://www.sos.ca.gov/elections/running-for-office/2010/pdf/independent-governor-lieutenant-governor-2010.pdf (accessed January 9, 2011).

———. https://www.sos.ca.gov/elections/statewide-elections/2014-primary/governor-lieutenant-governor-2014.htm (accessed February 2, 2015).

Silver, Thomas B. *Coolidge and the Historians.* Durham, NC: Carolina Academic Press, 1982.

Skerry, Peter. *Mexican-Americans: The Ambivalent Minority.* New York: Free Press, 1993.

———. "Mexican Immigration Is Different." In *The American Enterprise* (December 2000), 22.

Slaughterhouse Cases (1873) 83 U.S. 16.

Smiley, Jane. "The Morning After; the Mystery of Democracy Remains Unsolved." *Los Angeles Times.* October 9, 2003. B17.

Solomon, Deborah. "Big Man on Campus." *New York Times.* 2009. http://www.nytimes.com/2009/09/27/magazine/27fob-q4-t.html (accessed January 10, 2011).

Spalding, Matthew, and Patrick Garrity. *A Sacred Union of Citizens: George Washington's Farewell Address and the American Character.* Introduction by Daniel J. Boorstin. Lanham, MD: Rowman & Littlefield, 1996.

Squire, Peverill. "Legislative Professionalism and Membership Diversity in State Legislatures." *Legislative Studies Quarterly* 17, no. 1 (1992): 69–79.

———. "Uncontested Seats in State Legislative Elections." *Legislative Studies Quarterly* 25 (February 2000): 131–46.

Starr, Kevin. *Americans and the California Dream, 1850–1915.* New York: Oxford University Press, 1973.

———. *Material Dreams: Southern California through the 1920s.* New York: Oxford University Press, 1990.

———. *Endangered Dreams: The Great Depression in California.* New York: Oxford University Press, 1996.

———. *Embattled Dreams: California in War and Peace.* New York: Oxford University Press, 2002.

———. "Once the Dust Settles, Bring Back the Party of California." *Los Angeles Times,* October 9, 2003. B17.

"State Senate." *California Journal* 31, no. 2 (2000): 25–30.

Statistical Abstract of the United States. Washington, D.C.: United States Government Printing Office, 2000.

———. "Number of Local Governments, by Type." http://www.census.gov/compendia/statab/2011/tables/11s0427.pdf (accessed 2 February 2015).

Stewart, Jill. "Capitol Punishment," www.jillstewart.net/php/issues/issue1014.php (accessed November 2, 2003).

Strauss, Leo, and Joseph Cropsey, eds. *History of Political Philosophy.* 3rd ed. Chicago: University of Chicago Press, 1987.

Swain, Carol M., ed. *Debating Immigration.* New York: Cambridge University Press, 2007.

Taylor, Michael. "The Reign of S.F.'s Monarch of the Dailies; Hearst Media Empire Started with Examiner." *San Francisco Chronicle* (August 7, 1999): A9.

Tamaki, Julie. "Teacher Pension System Dumps Tobacco Stock." *Los Angeles Times* (June 8, 2000): A3.

Tarr, G. Alan. *Understanding State Constitutions.* Princeton, NJ: Princeton University Press, 1998.

Thernstrom, Stephan, ed. *The Harvard Encyclopedia of American Ethnic Groups.* Cambridge, MA: Harvard University Press, 1980.

Thernstrom, Stephan, and Abigail Thernstrom. *America in Black and White: One Nation, Indivisible.* New York: Simon and Schuster, 1997.

Tiebout, Charles. "A Pure Theory of Local Government Expenditures." *Journal of Political Economy* 64 (1956): 416–24.

Tocqueville, Alexis de. *Democracy in America.* Translated, edited, and with an introduction by Harvey C. Mansfield and Delba Winthrop. Chicago: University of Chicago Press, 2000.

———. *Tocqueville: Democracy in America.* Translated and edited by Arthur Goldhammer. New York: Library in America, 2004.

———. *Democracy in America.* Translated by James T. Schleifer and edited by Eduardo Nolla. Indianapolis, IN: Liberty Fund, 2010.

Truman, David B. *The Governmental Process: Political Interests and Public Opinion.* New York: Knopf, 1951.

———. *Democracy in America.* Edited with an introduction by Isaac Kramnick, translated by Gerald Bevan. London: Penguin Books, 2003.

Turner, Barry, ed. *The Statesman's Yearbook 2001.* London: Macmillan, 2001.

United States v. Oakland Cannabis Buyers' Cooperative (2001) 532 U.S. 483.

Van Oot, Torey. "Pérez Announces Leadership and Committee Assignments," *Sacramento Bee,* http://blogs.sacbee.com/capitolalertlatest/2010/12/perez-announces-dem-leadership.html (accessed February 2, 2015).

Vives, Ruben. "Ex-Bell Mayor's Store is Vandalized with Graffiti after Sentencing," *Los Angeles Times,* http://www.latimes.com/local/lanow/la-me-ln-ex-bell-mayor-store-graffiti-20140801-story.html (accessed January 29, 2015).

Voegeli, William. "Failed State." *Claremont Review of Books.* http://www.claremont.org/article/failed-state1/#.VM_t8mjF_To (accessed February 2, 2015).

Wahlke, John C., Heinz Eulau, William Buchanan, and LeRoy C. Ferguson. *The Legislative System.* New York: Wiley, 1962.

Walker, Jack. *Mobilizing Interest Groups in America.* Ann Arbor: University of Michigan Press, 1991.

Walters, Dan. "Legislature Risks Return to Elitism." *Fresno Bee* (June 27, 2000): A9.

———. "Governor a Reformer? Actions on Two Bills Belie Rhetoric." *Sacramento Bee* (October 6, 2004): A3.

———. "Brown's Budget Faces the State's Ugly Facts." *Orange County Register.* "Brown's Budget Faces the State's Ugly Facts," http://www.ocregister.com/articles/brown-283655-california-taxes.html (accessed February 2, 2015).

Warner, Susan. "Drug Firms Get a Dose of Disdain in this Election Year." *San Diego Union-Tribune* (September 2, 2000): C1.

Warren, Earl. *The Memoirs of Chief Justice Earl Warren.* Garden City, NY: Doubleday, 1977.

Weber, Max. "Bureaucracy." In *From Max Weber: Essays in Sociology.* Edited by H. H. Gerth and C. Wright Mills. New York: Oxford University Press, 1946, 196–244.

Weintraub, Daniel. "The War of the Californias." *Orange County Register.* September 30, 2003, B7.

Weissert, Carol S., and William S. Weissert. *Governing Health: The Politics of Health Policy.* Baltimore: Johns Hopkins University Press, 1996.

West, Thomas G. *Vindicating the Founders: Race, Sex, Class, and Justice in the Origins of America.* Lanham, MD: Rowman & Littlefield, 1997.

White, Louise G. *Political Analysis.* Pacific Grove, CA: Brooks/Cole, 1990.

Will, George F. "A Cure for California . . ." *Washington Post,* September 18, 2003, A23.

Wilson, E. Dotson, and Brian S. Ebbert. *California's Legislature.* Sacramento: California State Legislature, Office of the Chief Clerk of the Assembly, 1998.

Wilson, James Q. *Bureaucracy: What Government Agencies Do and Why They Do It.* New York: Basic Books, 1989.

Zigler, L. Harmon, and Hendrik van Dalen. "Interest Groups in the States." Pp. 122–60. In *Politics in the American States,* 2nd ed. Edited by Herbert Jacob and Kenneth N. Vines. Boston: Little, Brown, 1974.

Zimmerman, Janet. "Groups awaiting arrival of migrant detainees in Murrieta," *Orange County Register,* http://www.ocregister.com/articles/murrieta-627978-detainees-protesters.html (accessed January 25, 2015).

Index

About the Authors

Brian P. Janiskee received his PhD from Michigan State University and is professor and chair of the Department of Political Science at California State University, San Bernardino, where he is also a faculty member in the national security studies program. He has published several articles and books on such topics as special districts, crime policy, presidential elections, American colonial local government, and national security.

Ken Masugi received his PhD from the New School for Social Research and teaches for Johns Hopkins University's Center for Advanced Studies in American Government in Washington, D.C. He is editor of *Interpreting Tocqueville's "Democracy in America"* (described in the *American Political Science Review* as representing a "revolution in Tocqueville scholarship") and coeditor of four other books on modern and American political thought. A Senior Fellow of the Claremont Institute, Masugi is currently completing a monograph on *Democracy in America*.

CPSIA information can be obtained at www.ICGtesting.com
Printed in the USA
BVOW02s0425240615

405823BV00002B/2/P